WHY A CONTEMPORARY SHAKESPEARE?

The starting point of my project was when I learned both from television and in education, that Shakespeare is being increasingly dropped in schools and colleges because of the difficulty of the language. In some cases, I gather, they are given just a synopsis of the play, then the teacher or professor embroiders from his notes.

This is deplorable. We do not want Shakespeare progressively dropped because of superfluous difficulties that can be removed, skilfully, conservatively, keeping to every line of the text. Nor must we look at the question statically, for this state of affairs will worsen as time goes on and we get further away from the language of 400 years ago—difficult enough in all conscience now.

We must begin by ridding our mind of prejudice, i.e. we must not pre-judge the matter. A friend of mine on New York radio said that he was 'appalled' at the very idea; but when he heard my exposition of what was proposed he found it reasonable and convincing.

Just remember, I do not need it myself: *I live in the Elizabethan age*, Shakespeare's time, and have done for years, and am familiar with its language, and his. But even for me there are still difficulties—still more for modern people, whom I am out to help.

Who, precisely?

Not only students at school and in college, but all readers of Shakespeare. Not only those, but all viewers of the plays, in the theatre, on radio and television—actors too, who increasingly find pronunciation of the words difficult, particularly obsolete ones—and there are many, besides the difficulty of accentuation.

The difficulties are naturally far greater for non-English-speaking peoples. We must remember that he is our greatest asset, and that other peoples use him a great deal in learning our language. There are no Iron Curtains for him—though, during Mao's Cultural Revolution in China, he was prohibited. Now that the ban has been lifted, I learn that the Chinese in thousands flock to his plays.

Now, a good deal that was grammatical four hundred years ago is positively ungrammatical today. We might begin by removing what is no longer good grammar.

For example: plural subjects with a verb in the singular:

'*Is* Bushy, Green and the earl of Wiltshire dead?' Any objection to replacing 'is' correctly by 'are'? Certainly not. I notice that some modern editions already correct—

These high wild hills and rough uneven ways
Draw*s* out our miles and make*s* them wearisome

to 'draw' and 'make', quite sensibly. Then, why not go further and regularise this Elizabethan usage to modern, consistently throughout?

Similarly with archaic double negatives—'Nor shall you not think neither'—and double comparatives: 'this

THE CONTEMPORARY SHAKESPEARE

Edited by A. L. Rowse

King Henry IV Part I

Modern Text with Introduction

UNIVERSITY PRESS OF AMERICA

University Press of America,® Inc.

4720 Boston Way
Lanham, MD 20706

3 Henrietta Street
London WC2E 8LU England

Printed in the United States of America

Distributed to the trade by The Scribner Book Companies

Library of Congress Cataloging in Publication Data

Shakespeare, William, 1564-1616.
King Henry the Fourth, Part I.

(The Contemporary Shakespeare)
1. Henry IV, King of England, 1367-1413—Drama.
I. Rowse, A. L. (Alfred Leslie), 1903-
II. Title. III. Series: Shakespeare, William, 1564-
1616. Plays (University Press of America : Pbk. ed.)
PR2810.A2R69 1985 822.3'3 85-22715
ISBN 0-8191-3926-2 (pbk.)

This play is also available as part of Volume IV in a seven volume clothbound and slipcased set.

Book design by Leon Bolognese

is more worser than before. There are hundreds of instances of what is now just bad grammar to begin with.

There must be a few thousand instances of superfluous subjunctives to reduce to simplicity and sense. Today we use the subjunctive occasionally after 'if', when we say 'if it be'. But we mostly say today 'if it is'. Now Shakespeare has hundreds of subjunctives, not only after if, but after though, although, unless, lest, whether, until, till, etc.

I see no point whatever in retaining them. They only add superfluous trouble in learning English, when the great appeal of our language as a world-language is precisely that it has less grammar to learn than almost any. Russian is unbelievably complicated. Inflected languages—German is like Latin in this respect—are really rather backward; it has been a great recommendation that English has been more progressive in this respect in simplifying itself.

Now we can go further along this line: keep a few subjunctives, if you must, but reduce them to a minimum.

Let us come to the verb. It is a great recommendation to modern English that our verbs are comparatively simple to conjugate—unlike even French, for example. In the Elizabethan age there was a great deal more of it, and some of it inconsistent in modern usage. Take Shakespeare's,

'Where is thy husband now? Where be thy brothers?'

Nothing is lost by rendering this as we should today:

Where is your husband now? Where are your brothers?

And so on.

The second and third person singular—all those shouldsts and wouldsts, wilts and shalts, haths and doths, have become completely obsolete. Here a vast simplification may be effected—with no loss as far as I can see, and with advantages from several points of view.

For example, 'st' at the end of a word is rather difficult to say, and more difficult even for us when it is succeeded by a word beginning with 'th'. Try saying, 'Why usurpedst thou this?' Foreigners have the greatest difficulty in pronouncing our 'th' anyway—many never succeed in getting it round their tongues. Many of these tongue-twisters even for us proliferate in Shakespeare, and I see no objection to getting rid of *superfluous* difficulties. Much easier for people to say, 'Why did you usurp this?'—the same number of syllables too.

This pre-supposes getting rid of almost all thous and thees and thines. I have no objection to keeping a few here and there, if needed for a rhyme—even then they are sometimes not necessary.

Some words in Shakespeare have changed their meaning into the exact opposite: we ought to remove that stumbling-block. When Hamlet says, 'By heaven, I'll make a ghost of him that *lets* me', he means *stops*; and we should replace it by stops, or holds me. Shakespeare regularly uses the word 'owe' where we should say own: the meaning has changed. Take a line like, 'Thou dost here usurp the name thou ow'st not': we should say, 'You do here usurp the name you own not', with the bonus of getting rid of two ugly 'sts'.

The word 'presently' in the Elizabethan age did not mean in a few minutes or so, but immediately—instantly has the same number of syllables. 'Prevent' then had its Latin meaning, to go before, or forestall. Shakespeare frequently uses the word 'still' for always or ever.

Let us take the case of many archaic forms of words, simple one-syllable words that can be replaced without the slightest difference to the scansion: 'sith' for since, 'wrack' for wreck, 'holp' for helped, 'writ' for wrote, 'brake' for broke, 'spake' for spoke, 'bare' for bore, etc.

These give no trouble, nor do a lot of other words that he uses: 'repeal' for recall, 'reproof' for disproof, 'decline' for incline. A few words do give more trouble. The linguistic scholar, C. T. Onions, notes that it is sometimes difficult to give the precise meaning Shakespeare attaches to the word 'conceit'; it usually means thought, or fancy, or concept. I do not know that it ever has our meaning; actually the word 'conceited' with him means ingenious or fantastic, as 'artificial' with Elizabethans meant artistic or ingenious.

There is a whole class of words that have completely gone out, of which moderns do not know the meaning. I find no harm in replacing the word 'coistrel' by rascal, which is what it means—actually it has much the same sound—or 'coil' by fuss; we find 'accite' for summon, 'indigest' for formless. Hamlet's word 'reechy', for the incestuous kisses of his mother and her brother-in-law, has gone out of use: the nearest word, I suppose, would be reeky, but filthy would be a suitable modern equivalent.

In many cases it is extraordinary how little one would need to change, how conservative one could be. Take Hamlet's famous soliloquy, 'To be or not to be.' I find only two words that moderns would not know the meaning of, and one of those we might guess:

> . . .When he himself might his *quietus* make
> With a bare bodkin? Who would *fardels* bear. . .

'Quietus' means put paid; Elizabethans wrote the Latin 'quietus est' at the bottom of a bill that was paid—when it was—to say that it was settled. So that you could replace 'quietus' by settlement, same number of syllables, though not the same accentuation; so I would prefer to use the word acquittance, which has both.

'Fardels' means burdens; I see no objection to rendering, 'Who would burdens bear'—same meaning, same number of syllables, same accent: quite simple. I expect all the ladies to know what a bodkin is: a long pin, or skewer.

Now let us take something really difficult—perhaps the most difficult passage to render in all Shakespeare. It is the virtuoso comic piece describing all the diseases that horseflesh is heir to, in *The Taming of the Shrew*. The horse is Petruchio's. President Reagan tells me that this is the one Shakespearean part that he played—and a very gallant one too. In Britain last year we saw a fine performance of his on horseback in Windsor Park alongside of Queen Elizabeth II—very familiar ground to William Shakespeare and Queen Elizabeth I, as we know from *The Merry Wives of Windsor.*

Here is a headache for us: Petruchio's horse (not President Reagan's steed) was 'possessed with the glanders, and like to mose in the chine; troubled with the lampass, infected with the fashions, full of windgalls, sped with spavins, rayed with the yellows, past cure of the fives, stark spoiled with the staggers, begnawn with the bots; swayed in the back, and shoulder-shotten; near-legged before, and with a half-cheeked bit, and a headstall of sheep's leather', etc.

What on earth are we to make of that? No doubt it raised a laugh with Elizabethans, much more familiarly acquainted with horseflesh than we are; but I doubt if Hollywood was able to produce a nag for Reagan that qualified in all these respects.

Now, even without his horsemanship, we can clear one fence at the outset: 'mose in the chine'. Pages of superfluous commentary have been devoted to that word 'mose'. There was no such Elizabethan word: it was simply a printer's misprint for 'mourn', meaning dripping or running; so it suggests a running sore. You would need to consult the *Oxford English Dictionary*, compiled on historical lines, for some of the words, others like 'glanders' country folk know and we can guess.

So I would suggest a rendering something like this: 'possessed with glanders, and with a running sore in the back; troubled in the gums, and infected in the glands; full of galls in the fetlocks and swollen in the joints; yellow with jaundice, past cure of the strangles; stark spoiled with the staggers, and gnawed by worms; swayed in the back and shoulder put out; near-legged before, and with a half-cheeked bit and headgear of sheep's leather', etc. That at least makes it intelligible.

Oddly enough, one encounters the greatest difficulty with the least important words and phrases, Elizabethan expletives and malapropisms, or salutations like God 'ild you, Godden, for God shield you, Good-even, and so on. 'God's wounds' was Elizabeth I's favourite swearword; it appears frequently enough in Victorian novels as 'Zounds'— I have never heard anyone use it. The word 'Marry!', as in the phrase 'Marry come up!' has similarly gone out, though a very old gentleman at All Souls, Sir Charles Oman, had heard the phrase in the back-streets of Oxford just after the 1914-18 war. 'Whoreson' is frequent on the lips of coarse fellows in Shakespeare: the equivalent in Britain today would be bloody, in America (I suppose) s.o.b.

Relative pronouns, who and which: today we use who for persons, which for things. In Elizabethan times the two were hardly distinguished and were interchangeable. Provokingly Shakespeare used the personal relative 'who' more frequently for impersonal objects, rivers, buildings, towns; and then he no less frequently uses 'which' for persons. This calls out to be regularised for the modern reader.

Other usages are more confusing. The word 'cousin'

was used far more widely by the Elizabethans for their kin: it included nephews, for instance. Thus it is confusing in the English History plays to find a whole lot of nephews—like Richard III's, whom he had made away with in the Tower of London—referred to and addressed as cousins. That needs regularisation today, in the interests of historical accuracy and to get the relationship clear. The word 'niece' was sometimes used of a grandchild—in fact this is the word Shakespeare used in his will for his little grand-daughter Elizabeth, his eventual heiress who ended up as Lady Barnard, leaving money to her poor relations the Hathaways at Stratford. The Latin word *neptis*, from which niece comes also meant grandchild—Shakespeare's grammar-school education at Stratford was in Latin, and this shows you that he often thought of a word in terms of its Latin derivation.

Malapropisms, misuse of words, sometimes mistaking of meanings, are frequent with uneducated people, and sometimes not only with those. Shakespeare transcribed them from lower-class life to raise a laugh, more frequently than any writer for the purpose. They are an endearing feature of the talk of Mistress Quickly, hostess of the Boar's Inn in East Cheapside, and we have no difficulty in making out what she means. But in case some of us do, and for the benefit of non-native English speakers, I propose the correct word in brackets afterwards: 'You have brought her into such a canaries [quandary]. . .and she's as fartuous [virtuous] a civil, modest wife. . .'

Abbreviations: Shakespeare's text is starred—and in my view, marred—by innumerable abbreviations, which not only look ugly on the page but are sometimes difficult to pronounce. It is not easy to pronounce 'is't', or 'in't', or 'on't', and some others: if we cannot get rid of them altogether they should be drastically reduced. Similarly with 'i'th'', 'o'th'', with which the later plays are liberally bespattered, for "in the" or "of the."

We also have a quite unnecessary spattering of apostrophes in practically all editions of the plays—''d' for the past participle, e.g. 'gather'd'. Surely it is much better to regularise the past participle 'ed', e.g. gathered; and when the last syllable is, far less frequently, to be pronounced, then accent it, gatherèd.

This leads into the technical question of scansion, where a practising poet is necessary to get the accents right, to help the reader, and still more the actor. Most people will hardly notice that, very often, the frequent ending of words in 'ion', like reputation, has to be pronounced with two syllables at the end. So I propose to accent this when necessary, e.g. reputatiòn. I have noticed the word 'ocean' as tri-syllabic, so I accent it, to help, oceàn. A number of words which to us are monosyllables were pronounced as two: hour, fire, tired; I sometimes accent or give them a dieresis, either hoùr or fïre. In New England speech words like prayèr, thëre, are apt to be pronounced as two syllables—closer to Elizabethan usage (as with words like gotten) than is modern speech in Britain.

What I notice in practically all editions of Shakespeare's plays is that the editors cannot be relied on to put the accents in the right places. One play edited by a well known Shakespearean editor had, I observed, a dozen accents placed over the wrong syllables. This is understandable, for these people don't write poetry and do not know how to scan. William Shakespeare knew all about scanning, and you need to be both familiar with Elizabethan usage and a practising traditional poet to be able to follow him.

His earlier verse was fairly regular in scansion, mostly iambic pentameter with a great deal of rhyme. As time went on he loosened out, until there are numerous irregular lines—this leaves us much freer in the matter of modernising. Our equivalents should be rhythmically as close as possible, but a strait-jacket need be no part of the equipment. A good Shakespearean scholar tells us, 'there is no necessity for Shakespeare's lines to scan absolutely. He thought of his verse as spoken rather than written and of his rhythmic units in terms of the voice rather than the page.'

There is nothing exclusive or mandatory about my project. We can all read Shakespeare in any edition we like—in the rebarbative olde Englishe spelling of the First Folio, if we wish. Any number of conventional academic editions exist, all weighed down with a burden of notes, many of them superfluous. I propose to make most of them unnecessary—only one occasionally at the foot of very few pages. Let the text be freed of superfluous difficulties, remove obstacles to let it speak for itself, while adhering conservatively to every line.

We really do not need any more editions of the Plays on conventional lines—more than enough of those exist already. But *A Contemporary Shakespeare* on these lines—both revolutionary and conservative—should be a help to everybody all round the world—though especially for younger people, increasingly with time moving away from the language of 400 years ago.

INTRODUCTION

The two parts of *Henry IV* form the summit of Shakespeare's achievement in the English history plays so popular with Elizabethans. They found new inspiration in their country's past, opened up for them by the chronicles of Holinshed and Hall, of which Shakespeare made especial use. He also brought to its fullest development the mingling of history with comedy. These plays contain his greatest comic creation, the uproarious, disorderly, but verbally brilliant Falstaff (his verbal brilliance is Shakespeare's, and something of what he thought too is put into Falstaff's mouth).

This astonishing mixture of serious and sad with what is rollicking, ribald and bawdy, was the ultimate seed-bed which proliferated (via Sir Walter Scott) in the historical novel, in European and American literature. (The historically inspired novelist, William Faulkner, always carried a volume of Shakespeare in his suitcase on his journeys.) We may well regard Falstaff as the progenitor of the humorous types who abound subsequently in our literature.

As in all the English history plays we can observe the difference when Shakespeare is transcribing from the chronicle, his immediate source, plain history, and when he is writing, inspired, from his own creation—as in all the scenes whenever Falstaff appears. Sometimes the historical scenes also are inspired, when they appeal to the dramatist's imagination—as in the affecting interviews of the harassed King Henry IV and his errant son, Prince Hal; or the charming scene between Hotspur and his wife—almost the only thing that appeals to one in that roughneck character.

Hotspur has always appealed to the public, a plain soldierly type, very masculine, a man who lives for action: a brave fighting fool, with no political sense. He is also very rude to his ally, Glendower, leader of Welsh resistance, with whom he has no patience. Glendower is faithfully portrayed, as a very curious Celt: he was indeed something of a magus, with an undying charisma for the Welsh people. Shakespeare does justice to both—our sympathies lie with the more remarkable, the strange and unique Glendower.

Shakespeare halved the historic Hotspur's age to make him co-eval with Prince Hal and present the two in dramatic rivalry. It is when we come to the character of this young Prince of Wales that critics have found difficulty and expressed least sympathy. He is too subtle for them to understand, for he is a political type—needs must, if he is going to be a successful ruler. We now know, as the Victorians did not, that Prince Hal had a roistering youth—Shakespeare was close to the tradition and sources brought to light recently bear him out.

What did the young Prince see so much in the old reprobate, Falstaff? Well, he was always good for a laugh—and more, japes and jests, like the robbery on Gadshill, or the brilliant (and realistic) scenes at the Boar's Head, with Falstaff and Hal reversing roles and enacting an interview between father and son, King and Prince. It is to be noticed that the Prince is verbally a match for Falstaff: they always have an answer for each other. And, in spite of the bad company he keeps, the Prince's dignity is always safeguarded. He sees that the money robbed at Gadshill is restored; he is courteous to the deplorable women, Mistress

Quickly and Doll Tearsheet, where Falstaff is rude to them. The Prince is chivalrous and generous about Hotspur —who is not about him. The father-son relationship, between the King with all his cares and responsibilities, and his son and heir having a good fling and adding to his worries, is true to history—and to life. Shakespeare penetrated to the heart of the matter.

Most interesting to us today is the marvellously rich and true portrait of Elizabethan social life, particularly among the lower orders who haunted the taverns like the Boar's Head in Cheapside, or that near Rochester where the highway robbery at Gadshill was planned. Mistress Quickly, hostess of the Boar's Head, is an unforgettable character—first mistress too of the malapropisms which have done such good duty in English comedy. Falstaff's whore, Doll Tearsheet—what a genius Shakespeare had for naming his creations!—is hardly less memorable, with her foul-mouthed language, her quick temper and warm-heartedness: progenitress too of the sentimental good-hearted prostitute in literature. Pistol's inflated speech—he is often drunk, or otherwise crazy—parodies the rant of the earlier Elizabethan stage, with touches from Peele and Kyd, even Marlowe.

Altogether, the Rabelaisian speech of these characters offers special difficulty to the modern reader, particularly when it is the thieves' slang, of which Robert Greene showed his mastery in his 'Conny-catching' pamphlets. Shakespeare knew his way about in it—as probably in the life itself, lodging alone in the City, away from the family at Stratford. John Aubrey noticed that both Shakespeare and Ben Jonson went about observing people's 'humours'. Theatre life and folk gave another rich opportunity. What is so remarkable is the way the dramatist responded to every challenge, with artistic decorum: from the nobility of speech proper to the King and Prince Hal when speaking to his father and as a prince, to the realistic carriers and ostlers loading their goods for Charing Cross.

A modern editor has commented on the numerous colloquial abbreviations in these plays, and provides a list of them: 'a for he, an for if, an't for if it, in's for in his, on't for on it, i'th' for in the, o'th' for of the, on's for of his, or of its, ha' for have, 'has for he has, y'are for you are, etc. What is the point of retaining these forms, an offence to the eye, and a barrier to both reader and auditor? Here they are made intelligible in their modern form, along with words that are archaically unrecognisable. Elizabethan usage—Shakespeare particularly so—varied greatly, making no consistent distinction, between personal 'who' and impersonal 'which'. This has been regularised. So also the wide contemporary use of the term 'cousin' to include uncles, nephews, etc. apt to confuse the reader.

We catch Shakespeare in his own person, and in his profession, both in the theatre and as writer. Mistress Quickly is delighted by the scene put on by Falstaff and Prince Hal at the Boar's Head: 'O Jesu, he does it as like one of these harlotry players as ever I see!' We have references to the characters in the old morality plays so familiar in his youth, the Vice, Iniquity, Vanity. Fun is made of the inflated style of Lyly's *Euphues*—the platitudes expressed in pompous antitheses: 'though the camomile, the more it is trodden on the faster it grows, yet youth, the more it is wasted the sooner it wears.'

Elizabethan London is all round us, with the Prince appointing Falstaff to meet him at the Temple hall; or Lady Percy, whom her husband reproaches for not walking further than Finsbury—where the Fields were a favourite place of recreation—or for talking like a 'comfit-maker's wife', with her clichés 'in good sooth', and 'as true as I live.' The speech of Puritans is caricatured: 'God give thee the spirit of persuasion and him the ears of profiting', prays Falstaff, who says he could take to singing psalms like godly weavers at their work. Once more we hear of a ring—this time a thumb-ring—on an alderman. And Warwickshire is brought to the fore, with Falstaff's march by Daintry and Sutton Co'fil, the local pronunciations for Daventry and Sutton Coldfield.

Contemporary references attest the immense popularity of the character of Falstaff, and the printings of this play were equalled in number only by *Richard III.* For Falstaff Shakespeare originally employed the name of the historic Oldcastle, the Lollard. This was objected to by Lord Cobham, into whose family earlier the Lollard martyr had married. On the first Lord Hunsdon's death in 1596, Cobham succeeded briefly as Lord Chamberlain and patron of Shakespeare's Company. He did not last long, dying next year, to be followed by Hunsdon's son, the second Lord. This must have been more congenial, for the Cobhams belonged to the Cecil grouping, opposed by Essex and Southampton—Shakespeare's affiliation. Cobham lived in Blackfriars, as did the second Lord Hunsdon—familiar ground to Shakespeare and to become more so. We see that this Elizabethan circle was not a large one, its figures known to each other.

CHARACTERS

The King's Party

KING HENRY IV, formerly Henry Bolingbroke, son of John of Gaunt

HENRY (or HAL), Prince of Wales, the King's eldest son

LORD JOHN OF LANCASTER, a younger son of King Henry IV

EARL OF WESTMORLAND

SIR WALTER BLUNT

The Rebels

HENRY PERCY, Earl of Northumberland

HARRY HOTSPUR, his son

LADY PERCY (KATE), Hotspur's wife

THOMAS PERCY, Earl of Worcester

EDMUND, LORD MORTIMER

LADY MORTIMER, Mortimer's wife, daughter of Glendower

OWEN GLENDOWER, leader of Welsh resistance

EARL OF DOUGLAS

SIR RICHARD VERNON

RICHARD SCROOP, Archbishop of York

SIR MICHAEL, a member of the household of the Archbishop

SIR JOHN FALSTAFF

NED POINS

BARDOLPH

PETO

MISTRESS QUICKLY, hostess of the Boar's Head in Eastcheap

FRANCIS, a drawer

GADSHILL

VINTNER, TWO CARRIERS, CHAMBERLAIN, SHERIFF AND OFFICERS, OSTLER, MESSENGERS, TRAVELLERS, LORDS AND ATTENDANTS, SOLDIERS

Act I

SCENE I
Westminster. The palace.

Enter the King, Prince John of Lancaster,
Earl of Westmorland, Sir Walter Blunt, and others

KING HENRY
So shaken as we are, so wan with care,
Find we a time for frighted peace to pant,
And breathe short-winded accents of new broils
To be commenced in strands afar remote.
No more the thirsty entrance of this soil
Shall daub her lips with her own children's blood,
No more shall trenching war channel her fields,
Nor bruise her flowerets with the armèd hoofs
Of hostile paces. Those opposèd eyes,
Which—like the meteors of a troubled heaven—
All of one nature, of one substance bred,
Did lately meet in the intestine shock
And furious close of civil butchery,
Shall now, in mutual well-beseeming ranks,
March all one way, and be no more opposed
Against acquaintance, kindred, and allies.
The edge of war, like an ill-sheathèd knife,
No more shall cut its master. Therefore friends,
As far as to the sepulchre of Christ—
Whose soldier now, under whose blessed cross
We are impressèd and engaged to fight—
Forthwith a power of English shall we levy:
Whose arms were moulded in their mother's womb

To chase these pagans in those holy fields
Over whose acres walked those blessèd feet,
Which fourteen hundred years ago were nailed
For our advantage on the bitter cross.
But this our purpose now is twelve month old,
And fruitless it is to tell you we will go.
Therefòr we meet not now. Then let me hear
Of you, my gentle cousin Westmorland,
What yesternight our Council did decree
In forwarding this dear expedition.

WESTMORLAND

My liege, this haste was hot in questiòn,
And many limits of the charge set down
But yesternight; when all athwart there came
A post from Wales, laden with heavy news;
Whose worst was that the noble Mortimer—
Leading the men of Herefordshire to fight
Against the irregular and wild Glendower—
Was by the rude hands of that Welshman taken,
A thousand of his people butcherèd.
Upon whose dead corpses there was such misuse,
Such beastly shameless transformatiòn
By those Welshwomen done, as may not be
Without much shame retold or spoken of.

KING HENRY

It seems then that the tidings of this strife
Broke off our business for the Holy Land.

WESTMORLAND

This matched with others did, my gracious lord.
For more uneven and unwelcome news
Came from the north, and thus it did import.
On Holy-rood day, the gallant Hotspur there,
Young Harry Percy, and brave Archibald,
That ever valiant and approvèd Scot,
At Holmedon met, where they did spend
A sad and bloody hour—

As by discharge of their artillery,
And shape of likelihood, the news was told.
For he that brought them, in the very heat
And pride of their contention did take horse,
Uncertain of the issue any way.

KING HENRY

Here is a dear, a true industrious friend,
Sir Walter Blunt, new lighted from his horse,
Stained with the variation of each soil
Betwixt that Holmedon and this seat of ours,
And he has brought us smooth and welcome news.
The Earl of Douglas is discomfited.
Ten thousand bold Scots, two-and-twenty knights,
Balked in their own blood, did Sir Walter see
On Holmedon's plains. Of prisoners Hotspur took
Mordake, Earl of Fife and eldest son
To beaten Douglas, and the Earl of Atholl,
Of Murray, Angus, and Menteith.
And is not this an honourable spoil?
A gallant prize? Ha, cousin, is it not?

WESTMORLAND In faith,

It is a conquest for a prince to boast of.

KING HENRY

Yea, there you make me sad, and make me sin
In envy that my Lord Northumberland
Should be the father to so blest a son.
A son who is the theme of honour's tongue,
Among a grove the very straightest plant,
Who is sweet Fortune's minion and her pride.
While I by looking on the praise of him
See riot and dishonour stain the brow
Of my young Harry. O that it could be proved
That some night-tripping fairy had exchanged
In cradle-clothes our children where they lay,
And called mine Percy, his Plantagenet!
Then would I have his Harry, and he mine.

But leave him from my thoughts. What think you, cousin,
Of this young Percy's pride? The prisoners
Whom he in this adventure has surprised
To his own use he keeps, and sends me word
I shall have none but Mordake, Earl of Fife.

WESTMORLAND
This is his uncle's teaching. This is Worcester,
Malevolent to you in all aspècts,
Which makes him prune himself, and bristle up
The crest of youth against your dignity.

KING HENRY
But I have sent for him to answer this,
And for this cause awhile we must neglect
Our holy purpose to Jerusalem.
Cousin, on Wednesday next our Council we
Will hold at Windsor, so inform the lords.
But come yourself with speed to us again,
For more is to be said and to be done
Than out of anger can be utterèd.

WESTMORLAND
I will, my liege.

Exeunt

SCENE II
Prince Henry's house.

Falstaff asleep: Enter Prince Henry waking him

FALSTAFF Now Hal, what time of day is it, lad?

PRINCE HAL You are so fat-witted with drinking old sack, and unbuttoning after supper, and sleeping upon benches after noon, that you have forgotten to demand that truly which you would truly know. What the devil have you to do with the time of the day? Unless hours were cups of sack, and minutes capons, and clocks the tongues of bawds, and dials the signs of brothels, and the blessed sun itself a fair hot wench in flame-coloured taffeta, I see no reason why you should be so superfluous to demand the time of the day.

FALSTAFF Indeed, you come near me now, Hal. For we that take purses go by the moon and the seven stars, and not 'by Phoebus, he, that wandering knight so fair'. And I pray you sweet wag, when you are king, as God save your grace—majesty I should say, for grace you will have none—

PRINCE HAL What, none?

FALSTAFF No, by my word, not so much as will serve to be prologue to an egg and butter.

PRINCE HAL Well, how then? Come, roundly, roundly.

FALSTAFF Well then, sweet wag, when you are king let not us that are squires of the night's body be called thieves of the day's beauty. Let us be Diana's foresters, gentlemen of the shade, minions of the moon. And let men say we are men of good government, being governed as the sea is by our noble and chaste mistress the moon, under whose countenance we steal.

PRINCE HAL You say well, and it holds well too, for the fortune of us that are the moon's men does ebb and flow like the sea, being governed as the sea is, by the moon. As for proof? Now, a purse of gold most resolutely snatched on Monday night, and most dissolutely spent on Tuesday morning, got with swearing 'Lay by!', and spent with crying 'Bring in!', now in as low an ebb as the foot of the ladder, and by and by in as high a flow as the ridge of the gallows.

FALSTAFF By the Lord, you say true, lad—and is not my hostess of the tavern a most sweet wench?

PRINCE HAL As the honey of Hybla, my old lad of the castle. And is not a buff jerkin a most sweet robe of durance?

FALSTAFF How now, how now, mad wag? What, in your quips and your quiddities? What a plague have I to do with a buff jerkin?

PRINCE HAL Why, what a pox have I to do with my hostess of the tavern?

FALSTAFF Well, you have called her to a reckoning many a time and oft.

PRINCE HAL Did I ever call for you to pay your part?

FALSTAFF No, I'll give you your due, you have paid all there.

PRINCE HAL Yea, and elsewhere, so far as my coin would stretch, and where it would not I have used my credit.

FALSTAFF Yea, and so used it that were it not here apparent that you are heir apparent—but I pray, sweet wag, shall there be gallows standing in England when you are king? And resolution thus fobbed off as it is with the rusty curb of old Father Antic the law? Do not you when you are king hang a thief.

PRINCE HAL No, you shall.

FALSTAFF Shall I? O rare! By the Lord, I'll be a brave judge!

PRINCE HAL You judge false already! I mean you shall have the hanging of the thieves, and so become a rare hangman.

FALSTAFF Well, Hal, well! And in some sort it chimes with my humour—as well as waiting in the Court, I can tell you.

PRINCE HAL For obtaining of suits?

FALSTAFF Yea, for obtaining of suits, whereof the hangman has no lean wardrobe. God, I am as melancholy as a tom cat, or a lugged bear.

PRINCE HAL Or an old lion, or a lover's lute.

FALSTAFF Yea, or the drone of a Lincolnshire bagpipe.

PRINCE HAL What say you to a hare, or the melancholy of Moorditch?

FALSTAFF You have the most unsavoury similes, and are indeed the most comparative rascalliest sweet young prince. But Hal, I pray you trouble me no more with vanity. I would to God you and I knew where a commodity of good names were to be bought. An old lord of the Council rated me the other day in the street about you, sir. But I marked him not, and yet he talked very wisely; but I regarded him not, and yet he talked wisely—and in the street too.

PRINCE HAL You did well, for wisdom cries out in the streets and no man regards it.

FALSTAFF O, you have damnable iteration, and are indeed able to corrupt a saint. You have done much harm upon me, Hal, God forgive you for it. Before I knew you, Hal, I knew nothing; and now am I, if a man should speak truly, little better than one of the wicked. I must give over this life, and I will give it over. By the Lord, if I do not I am a villain. I'll be damned for never a king's son in Christendom.

PRINCE HAL Where shall we take a purse tomorrow, Jack?

FALSTAFF Zounds,[1] where you will lad, I'll make one; if I do not, call me a villain and degrade me.

PRINCE HAL I see a good amendment of life in you, from praying to purse-taking.

FALSTAFF Why Hal, 'tis my vocation, Hal. It is no sin for a man to labour in his vocation.

Enter Poins

Poins! Now shall we know if Gadshill has set a match! O, if men were to be saved by merit, what hole in hell were hot enough for him? This is the most omnipotent villain that ever cried 'Stand!' to a true man.

PRINCE HAL Good morrow, Ned.

POINS Good morrow, sweet Hal. What says Monsieur Remorse? What says Sir John Sack—and Sugar? Jack!

---

[1]Short for God's wounds, Elizabeth I's usual expletive.

How agree the devil and you about your soul, that you sold him on Good Friday last, for a cup of Madeira and a cold capon's leg?

PRINCE HAL Sir John stands to his word, the devil shall have his bargain; for he was never yet a breaker of proverbs. He will give the devil his due.

POINS Then are you damned for keeping your word with the devil.

PRINCE HAL Else he had been damned for cozening the devil.

POINS But my lads, my lads, tomorrow morning, by four o'clock early at Gad's Hill, there are pilgrims going to Canterbury with rich offerings and traders riding to London with fat purses. I have masks for you all—you have horses for yourselves. Gadshill lies tonight in Rochester. I have bespoken supper tomorrow night in Eastcheap. We may do it as secure as sleep. If you will go, I will stuff your purses full of crowns. If you will not, tarry at home and be hanged.

FALSTAFF Hear you, Edward, if I tarry at home and go not, I'll hang you for going.

POINS You will, chaps?

FALSTAFF Hal, will you make one?

PRINCE HAL Who I? Rob? I a thief? Not I, by my faith.

FALSTAFF There's neither honesty, manhood, nor good fellowship in you. You came not of the blood royal, if you dare not stand for ten shillings.

PRINCE HAL Well then, once in my days I'll be a madcap.

FALSTAFF Why, that's well said.

PRINCE HAL Well, come what will, I'll tarry at home.

FALSTAFF By the Lord, I'll be a traitor then, when you are king.

PRINCE HAL I care not.

POINS Sir John, I pray you leave the Prince and me alone. I will lay him down such reasons for this adventure that he shall go.

FALSTAFF Well, God give you the spirit of persuasion, and him the ears of profiting, that what you speak may move, and what he hears may be believed: that the true prince may—for recreation sake—prove a false thief, for the poor abuses of the time want countenance. Farewell, you shall find me in Eastcheap.

PRINCE HAL Farewell, the latter spring! Farewell, Allhallows' summer! *Exit Falstaff*

POINS Now my good sweet honey lord, ride with us tomorrow. I have a jest to execute that I cannot manage alone. Falstaff, Bardolph, Peto, and Gadshill shall rob those men that we have already waylaid—yourself and I will not be there. And when they have the booty, if you and I do not rob them—cut this head off from my shoulders.

PRINCE HAL How shall we part with them in setting forth?

POINS Why, we will set forth before or after them, and appoint them a place of meeting—wherein it is at our pleasure to fail. And then will they adventure upon the exploit themselves, which they shall have no sooner achieved but we'll set upon them.

PRINCE HAL Yea, but 'tis likely that they will know us by our horses, by our habits, and by every other appointment to be ourselves.

POINS Tut, our horses they shall not see, I'll tie them in the wood. Our masks we will change after we leave them. And, sir, I have cases of buckram for the chance, to hide our noted outward garments.

PRINCE HAL Yea, but I doubt they will be too hard for us.

POINS Well, for two of them, I know them to be as truebred cowards as ever turned back; and for the third, if he fights longer than he sees reason, I'll forswear arms. The virtue of this jest will be the incomprehensible lies that this same fat rogue will tell us when we meet at supper. How thirty at least he fought with, what wards, what blows, what extremities he endured, and in the disproof of this lives the jest.

PRINCE HAL Well, I'll go with you. Provide us all things necessary and meet me tomorrow night in Eastcheap. There I'll sup. Farewell.

POINS Farewell, my lord. *Exit*

PRINCE HAL
I know you all, and will awhile uphold
The unyoked humour of your idleness.
Yet herein will I imitate the sun,
Which does permit the base contagious clouds
To smother up its beauty from the world,
That when it pleases again to be itself,
Being wanted, it may be more wondered at
By breaking through the foul and ugly mists
Of vapours that did seem to strangle it.
If all the year were playing holidays,
To sport would be as tedious as to work;
But when they seldom come, they wished-for come,
And nothing pleases but rare accidents.
So when this loose behaviour I throw off,
And pay the debt I never promisèd,
By how much better than my word I am,
By so much shall I falsify men's hopes.
And like bright metal on a sullen ground,
My reformation, glittering o'er my fault,
Shall show more goodly, and attract more eyes
Than that which has no foil to set it off.
I'll so offend, to make offence a skill,
Redeeming time when men think least I will.

Exit

SCENE III
Windsor Castle.

Enter the King, Northumberland, Worcester, Hotspur, Sir Walter Blunt, and others

KING HENRY
My blood has been too cold and temperate,
Unapt to stir at these indignities,
And you have found me—for accordingly
You tread upon my patience. But be sure
I will from henceforth rather be myself,
Mighty, and to be feared, than my condition,
Which has been smooth as oil, soft as young down,
And therefore lost that title of respect
Which the proud soul never pays but to the proud.

WORCESTER
Our house, my sovereign liege, little deserves
The scourge of greatness to be used on it,
And that same greatness too which our own hands
Have helped to make so portly.

NORTHUMBERLAND My lord—

KING HENRY
Worcester, get you gone, for I do see
Danger and disobedience in your eye.
O sir, your presence is too pèremptory,
And majesty might never yet endure
The moody frontier of a servant brow.
You have good leave to leave us. When we need
Your use and counsel we shall send for you.
Exit Worcester
(*To Northumberland*) You were about to speak.

NORTHUMBERLAND Yea, my good lord.
Those prisoners in your highness' name demanded,
Which Harry Percy here at Holmedon took,
Were, as he says, not with such strength denied

As is delivered to your majesty.
Either envy therefore, or misunderstanding,
Is guilty of this fault, and not my son.

HOTSPUR

My liege, I did deny no prisoners.
But I remember when the fight was done,
When I was dry with rage and èxtreme toil,
Breathless and faint, leaning upon my sword,
Came there a certain lord, neat and trimly dressed,
Fresh as a bridegroom, and his chin new reaped
Showed like a stubble-land at harvest-home.
He was perfumèd like a milliner,
Between his finger and his thumb he held
A perfume-box, which ever and anon
He gave his nose, and took it away again—
Which therewith angry, when it next came there,
Took it in snuff. And still he smiled and talked.
And as the soldiers bore dead bodies by,
He called them untaught knaves, unmannerly,
To bring a slovenly unhandsome corpse
Between the wind and his nobility.
With many holiday and lady terms
He questioned me; among the rest demanded
My prisoners in your majesty's behalf.
I then, all smarting with my wounds being cold,
To be so pestered with a popinjay,
Out of my grief and my impatiènce
Answered neglectingly, I know not what—
He should, or he should not, for he made me mad
To see him shine so brisk, and smell so sweet,
And talk so like a waiting-gentlewoman
Of guns, and drums, and wounds, God save the mark!
And telling me the sovereignest thing on earth
Was parmaceti for an inward bruise,
And that it was great pity, so it was,
This villainous saltpetre should be digged

Out of the bowels of the harmless earth,
Which many a good tall fellow had destroyed
So cowardly; and but for these vile guns
He would himself have been a soldier.
This bald unjointed chat of his, my lord,
I answered indirectly, as I said,
And I beseech you, let not his report
Come current for an accusatiòn
Between my love and your high majesty.

BLUNT

The circumstance considered, good my lord,
Whatever Lord Harry Percy then had said
To such a person, and in such a place,
At such a time, with all the rest retold,
May reasonably die; and never rise
To do him wrong, or any way impeach
What then he said, so he unsays it now.

KING HENRY

Why, yet he does deny his prisoners,
But with proviso and exceptiòn,
That we at our own charge shall ransom straight
His brother-in-law, the foolish Mortimer.
Who, on my soul, has wilfully betrayed
The lives of those that he did lead to fight
Against that great magician, damned Glendower,
Whose daughter, as we hear, the Earl of March
Has lately married. Shall our coffers then
Be emptied to redeem a traitor home?
Shall we buy treason, and bargain then with fears
When they have lost and forfeited themselves?
No, on the barren mountains let him starve.
For I shall never hold that man my friend
Whose tongue shall ask me for one penny cost
To ransom home revolted Mortimer.

HOTSPUR
Revolted Mortimer!
He never did fall off, my sovereign liege,
But by the chance of war. To prove that true
Needs no more but one tongue for all those wounds—
Those mouthèd wounds, which valiantly he took,
When on the gentle Severn's sedgy bank,
In single opposition hand to hand,
He did confound the best part of an hour
In changing hardihood with great Glendower.
Three times they breathed, and three times did they drink
Upon agreement of swift Severn's flood,
Which then affrighted with their bloody looks
Ran fearfully among the trembling reeds,
And hid its crisp head in the hollow bank,
Bloodstained with these valiant combatants.
Never did bare and rotten policy
Colour its working with such deadly wounds;
And never could the noble Mortimer
Receive so many, and all willingly.
Then let not him be slandered with revolt.

KING HENRY
You do belie him, Percy, you do belie him,
He never did encounter with Glendower.
I tell you, he durst as well have met the devil alone
As Owen Glendower for an enemy.
Are you not ashamed? But sir, henceforth
Let me not hear you speak of Mortimer.
Send me your prisoners with the speediest means—
Or you shall hear in such a kind from me
As will displease you. My Lord Northumberland:
We license your departure with your son.
Send us your prisoners, or you will hear of it.

Exit the King with Blunt and train

HOTSPUR

And if the devil comes and roars for them
I will not send them. I will after straight
And tell him so, for I will ease my heart,
Albeit I make a hazard of my head.

NORTHUMBERLAND

What? Drunk with choler? Stay, and pause awhile,
Here comes your uncle.

Enter Worcester

HOTSPUR Speak of Mortimer?
Zounds, I will speak of him, and let my soul
Want mercy if I do not join with him.
Yea, on his part I'll empty all these veins
And shed my dear blood, drop by drop in the dust,
But I will lift the down-trodden Mortimer
As high in the air as this unthankful King,
As this ingrate and cankered Bolingbroke.

NORTHUMBERLAND

Brother, the King has made your nephew mad.

WORCESTER

Who struck this heat up after I was gone?

HOTSPUR

He will indeed have all my prisoners,
And when I urged the ransom once again
Of my wife's brother, then his cheek looked pale;
And on my face he turned an eye of death,
Trembling even at the name of Mortimer.

WORCESTER

I cannot blame him. Was not he proclaimed,
By Richard that dead is, the next of blood?

NORTHUMBERLAND

He was, I heard the proclamatiòn.
And then it was, when the unhappy King—
Whose wrongs in us God pardon!—did set forth

Upon his Irish expeditiòn;
From whence he, intercepted, did return
To be deposed, and shortly murderèd.

WORCESTER

And for whose death we in the world's wide mouth
Live scandalized and foully spoken of.

HOTSPUR

But soft, I pray you, did King Richard then
Proclaim my kinsman Edmund Mortimer
Heir to the crown?

NORTHUMBERLAND He did, myself did hear it.

HOTSPUR

Nay then, I cannot blame his cousin King
That wished him on the barren mountains starve.
But shall it be that you that set the crown
Upon the head of this forgetful man,
And for his sake wear the detested blot
Of murderous subornation—shall it be
That you a world of curses undergo,
Being the agents, or base second means,
The cords, the ladder, or the hangman rather?
O pardon me, that I descend so low,
To show the line and the predicament
Wherein you range under this subtle King!
Shall it for shame be spoken in these days,
Or fill up chronicles in time to come,
That men of your nobility and power
Did gage them both in an unjust behalf—
As both of you, God pardon it, have done—
To put down Richard, that sweet lovely rose,
And plant this thorn, this canker Bolingbroke?
And shall it in more shame be further spoken,
That you are fooled, discarded, shaken off
By him for whom these shames you underwent?
No, yet time serves wherein you may redeem
Your banished honours, and restore yourselves

Into the good thoughts of the world again.
Revenge the jeering and disdained contempt
Of this proud King, who studies day and night
To answer all the debt he owes to you,
Even with the bloody payment of your deaths.
Therefore, I say—

WORCESTER Peace, cousin, say no more.
And now I will unclasp a secret book,
And to your quick-conceiving discontents
I'll read you matter deep and dangerous—
As full of peril and adventurous spirit
As to over-walk a current roaring loud
On the unsteadfast footing of a spear.

HOTSPUR
If he falls in, good night, or sink, or swim!
Send danger from the east unto the west,
So honour cross it from the north to south,
And let them grapple. O, the blood more stirs
To rouse a lion than to start a hare!

NORTHUMBERLAND
Imagination of some great exploit
Drives him beyond the bounds of patiènce.

HOTSPUR
By heaven, I think it were an easy leap
To pluck bright honour from the pale-faced moon,
Or dive into the bottom of the deep,
Where fathom-line could never touch the ground,
And pluck up drownèd honour by the locks—
So he that does redeem it thence might wear
Without corrival all its dignities.
But out upon this half-faced fellowship!

WORCESTER
He apprehends a world of figures here,
But not the form of what he should attend.
Good cousin, give me audience for a while.

HOTSPUR
I cry you mercy.
WORCESTER Those same noble Scots
That are your prisoners—
HOTSPUR I'll keep them all!
By God he shall not have a Scot of them,
No, if a scot would save his soul he shall not.
I'll keep them, by this hand!
WORCESTER You start away,
And lend no ear unto my purposes.
Those prisoners you shall keep—
HOTSPUR Nay, I will. That's flat!
He said he would not ransom Mortimer,
Forbade my tongue to speak of Mortimer;
But I will find him when he lies asleep,
And in his ear I'll holla 'Mortimer!'
Nay, I'll have a starling shall be taught to speak
Nothing but 'Mortimer', and give it him
To keep his anger still in motiòn.
WORCESTER
Hear you, cousin, a word.
HOTSPUR
All studies here I solemnly defy,
Save how to gall and pinch this Bolingbroke.
And that same sword-and-buckler Prince of Wales—
But that I think his father loves him not
And would be glad he met with some mischance—
I would have him poisoned with a pot of ale.
WORCESTER
Farewell, kinsman. I'll talk to you
When you are better tempered to attend.
NORTHUMBERLAND
Why, what a wasp-stung and impatient fool
Are you to break into this woman's mood,
Tying your ear to no tongue but your own!

HOTSPUR

Why, look you, I am whipped and scourged with rods,
Nettled, and stung with hornets, when I hear
Of this vile politician Bolingbroke.
In Richard's time—what do you call the place?
A plague upon it, it is in Gloucestershire.
'Twas where the madcap Duke his uncle kept—
His uncle York—where I first bowed my knee
Unto this king of smiles, this Bolingbroke—
God, when you and he came back from Ravenspurgh—

NORTHUMBERLAND

At Berkeley Castle.

HOTSPUR

You say true.
Why, what a candy deal of courtesy
This fawning greyhound then did proffer me!
'Look when his infant fortune came to age',
And 'gentle Harry Percy', and 'kind cousin'.
O, the devil take such cozeners—God forgive me!
Good uncle, tell your tale. I have done.

WORCESTER

Nay, if you have not, to it again,
We will stay your leisure.

HOTSPUR I have done, in faith.

WORCESTER

Then once more to your Scottish prisoners.
Deliver them up without their ransom straight,
And make the Douglas' son your only means
For power in Scotland. Which, for divers reasons
Which I shall send you written, be assured
Will easily be granted. (*To Northumberland*) You my lord,
Your son in Scotland being thus employed,
Shall secretly into the bosom creep
Of that same noble prelate well-beloved,
The Archbishop.

HOTSPUR Of York, is it not?
WORCESTER True, who bears hard
His brother's death at Bristol, the Lord Scroop.
I speak not this in estimatiòn,
As what I think might be, but what I know
Is ruminated, plotted, and set down—
And only stays but to behold the face
Of that occasion that shall bring it on.

HOTSPUR
I smell it! Upon my life it will do well!

NORTHUMBERLAND
Before the game is afoot you ever let slip.

HOTSPUR
Why, it cannot choose but be a noble plot;
And then the power of Scotland, and of York,
To join with Mortimer, ha?

WORCESTER And so they shall.

HOTSPUR
In faith it is exceedingly well aimed.

WORCESTER
It is no little reason bids us speed,
To save our heads by raising of a head.
For, bear ourselves as even as we can,
The King will always think him in our debt,
And think we think ourselves unsatisfied,
Till he has found a time to pay us home.
And see already how he does begin
To make us strangers to his looks of love.

HOTSPUR
He does, he does, we'll be revenged on him.

WORCESTER
Cousin, farewell. No further go in this
Than I by letters shall direct your course.
When time is ripe, which will be suddenly,
I'll steal to Glendower, and Lord Mortimer,
Where you, and Douglas, and our powers at once,

As I will fashion it, shall happily meet
To bear our fortunes in our own strong arms,
Which now we hold at much uncertainty.

NORTHUMBERLAND

Farewell, good brother. We shall thrive, I trust.

HOTSPUR

Uncle, adieu. O, let the hours be short,
Till fields, and blows, and groans applaud our sport!

Exeunt

Act II

SCENE I
Rochester. An inn yard.

Enter a Carrier with a lantern in his hand

FIRST CARRIER Heigh-ho! If it is not four by the day I'll be hanged. Charles's Wain is over the new chimney, and yet our horse not packed. What, Ostler!

OSTLER *(within)* Anon, anon.

FIRST CARRIER I pray you, Tom, beat Cut's saddle, put a few flocks in the saddle-bow; poor jade is wrung in the withers out of all bearing.

Enter another Carrier

SECOND CARRIER Peas and beans are as dank here as a dog, and that is the next way to give poor jades the worms. This house is turned upside down since Robin Ostler died.

FIRST CARRIER Poor fellow never joyed since the price of oats rose, it was the death of him.

SECOND CARRIER I think this is the most villainous house in all London road for fleas, I am stung like a tench.

FIRST CARRIER Like a tench! By the mass, there is never a king Christian could be better bit than I have been since the first cock crow.

SECOND CARRIER Why, they will allow us never a jordan, and then we leak in your chimney, and your wine breeds fleas like a lamprey.

FIRST CARRIER What, Ostler! Come away, and be hanged, come away!

SECOND CARRIER I have a gammon of bacon, and two roots of ginger, to be delivered as far as Charing Cross.

FIRST CARRIER God's body! The turkeys in my pannier are quite starved. What, Ostler! A plague on you, have you never an eye in your head? Can you not hear? If it were not as good deed as drink to break the pate on you, I am a very villain. Come, and be hanged! Have you no faith in you?

Enter Gadshill

GADSHILL Good morrow, carriers, what's o'clock?

FIRST CARRIER I think it is two o'clock.

GADSHILL I pray lend me your lantern, to see my gelding in the stable.

FIRST CARRIER Nay, by God, soft! I know a trick worth two of that, in faith.

GADSHILL I pray you lend me yours.

SECOND CARRIER Ay, when? Can tell? Lend me your lantern, says he! I'll see you hanged first.

GADSHILL Carrier, what time do you mean to come to London?

SECOND CARRIER Time enough to go to bed with a candle, I warrant you! Come, neighbour Mugs, we'll call up the gentlemen, they will along with company, for they have great charge. *Exeunt Carriers*

GADSHILL What ho! Chamberlain!

Enter Chamberlain

CHAMBERLAIN 'At hand, says pick-purse.'

GADSHILL That's even as fair as 'At hand, says the chamberlain', for you vary no more from picking of purses than giving direction does from labouring. You lay the plot how.

CHAMBERLAIN Good morrow, Master Gadshill. It holds current what I told you yesternight. There's a franklin in the Weald of Kent has brought three hundred marks with him in gold. I heard him tell it to one of his company last night at supper, a kind of auditor, one that has abundance of baggage too, God knows what. They are up already, and call for eggs and butter. They will away at once.

GADSHILL Sir, if they meet not with Saint Nicholas' clerks, I'll give you this neck.

CHAMBERLAIN No, I'll none of it, I pray you keep that for the hangman, for I know you worship Saint Nicholas, as truly as a man of falsehood may.

GADSHILL What talk you to me of the hangman? If I hang, I'll make a fat pair of gallows. For if I hang, old Sir John hangs with me, and you know he is no starveling. Tut, there are other Trojans that you dream not of, which for sport sake are content to do the profession some grace; that would, if matters should be looked into, for their own credit sake make all whole. I am joined with no footpads, no long-staff sixpenny strikers, none of these mad mustached purple-hued drunks, but with nobility and tranquillity, burgomasters and great ones—such as can hold in, such as will strike sooner than speak, and speak sooner than drink, and drink sooner than pray. And yet, zounds, I lie; for they pray continually to their saint the commonwealth, or rather not pray to her, but prey on her, for they ride up and down on her, and make her their boots.[1]

CHAMBERLAIN What, the commonwealth their boots? Will she hold water out in foul way?

[1]The punning innuendo here is on boots and booty.

GADSHILL She will, she will, justice has liquored her. We steal as in a castle, cock-sure. We have the receipt of fern-seed, we walk invisible.

CHAMBERLAIN Nay, by my faith, I think you are more beholden to the night than to fern-seed for your walking invisible.

GADSHILL Give me your hand, you shall have a share in our purchase, as I am a true man.

CHAMBERLAIN Nay, rather let me have it as you are a false thief.

GADSHILL Go to, *homo* is a common name to all men. Bid the ostler bring my gelding out of the stable. Farewell, you muddy knave. *Exeunt*

Scene II
The road by Gadshill.

Enter Prince and Poins

POINS Come, shelter, shelter! I have removed Falstaff's horse, and he frets like a gummed velvet.

PRINCE HALL Stand close!

They hide
Enter Falstaff

FALSTAFF Poins! Poins, and be hanged! Poins!

PRINCE HAL *(coming forward)* Peace, you fat-kidneyed rascal, what a brawling do you keep!

FALSTAFF Where's Poins, Hal?

PRINCE HAL He has walked up to the top of the hill. I'll go seek him.

He steps to one side

FALSTAFF I am accursed to rob in that thief's company. The rascal has removed my horse and tied him I know not where. If I travel but four foot by the square further afoot, I shall break my wind. Well, I doubt not but to die a fair death for all this, if I escape hanging for killing that rogue. I have forsworn his company hourly any time this two-and-twenty years, and yet I am bewitched with the rogue's company. If the rascal has not given me medicines to make me love him, I'll be hanged. It could not be else. I have drunk medicines. Poins! Hal! A plague upon you both! Bardolph! Peto! I'll starve ere I'll rob a foot further—if it were not as good a deed as drink to turn true man, and to leave these rogues, I am the veriest varlet that ever chewed with a tooth. Eight yards of uneven ground is threescore-and-ten miles afoot with me, and the stony-hearted villains know it well enough. A plague upon it when thieves cannot be true one to another!

They whistle

Whew! A plague upon you all. Give me my horse, you rogues, give me my horse and be hanged!

PRINCE HAL (*coming forward*) Peace, you fat-guts, lie down, lay your ear close to the ground and listen if you can hear the tread of travellers.

FALSTAFF Have you any levers to lift me up again, being down? God, I'll not bear my own flesh so far afoot again for all the coin in your father's exchequer. What a plague mean you to colt [trick] me thus?

PRINCE HAL You lie, you are not colted, you are uncolted.

FALSTAFF I pray good Prince Hal, help me to my horse, good king's son.

PRINCE HAL Out, you rogue, shall I be your ostler?

FALSTAFF Hang yourself in your own heir-apparent garters! If I am taken, I'll peach for this. If I have not ballads made on you all, and sung to filthy tunes, let a cup of sack be my poison. When a jest is so forward—and afoot too—I hate it!

Enter Gadshill, Bardolph, and Peto

GADSHILL Stand!

FALSTAFF So I do, against my will.

POINS O, 'tis our mate, I know his voice. Bardolph, what news?

BARDOLPH Disguise, on with your masks, there's money of the King's coming down the hill. 'Tis going to the King's exchequer.

FALSTAFF You lie, you rogue, 'tis going to the King's tavern.

GADSHILL There's enough to make us all—

FALSTAFF To be hanged.

PRINCE HAL Sirs, you four shall confront them in the narrow lane. Ned Poins and I will walk lower—if they escape from your encounter, then they light on us.

PETO How many are there of them?

GADSHILL Some eight or ten.

FALSTAFF Zounds, will they not rob us?

PRINCE HAL What, a coward, Sir John Paunch?

FALSTAFF Indeed, I am not John of Gaunt your grandfather, but yet no coward, Hal.

PRINCE HAL Well, we leave that to the proof.

POINS Sir Jack, your horse stands behind the hedge. When you need him, there you shall find him. Farewell, and stand fast!

FALSTAFF Now cannot I strike him, if I should be hanged.

PRINCE HAL (*aside to Poins*) Ned, where are our disguises?

POINS Here, hard by, stand close. *Exeunt Prince and Poins*

FALSTAFF Now, my masters, happy man be his lot, say I. Every man to his business.

Enter the Travellers

FIRST TRAVELLER Come, neighbour, the boy shall lead our horses down the hill. We'll walk afoot awhile and ease our legs.

THIEVES Stand!

SECOND TRAVELLER Jesus bless us!

FALSTAFF Strike, down with them, cut the villains' throats! Ah, bloody caterpillars, bacon-fed knaves, they hate us youth! Down with them, fleece them!

FIRST TRAVELLER O, we are undone, both we and ours for ever!

FALSTAFF Hang you, potbellied knaves, are you undone? No, you fat chuffs, I would your store were here! On, bacons, on! What, you knaves, young men must live! You are grandjurors, are you? We'll jury you, faith.

Here they rob them and bind them

Exeunt

Enter the Prince and Poins, disguised

PRINCE HAL The thieves have bound the true men. Now, could you and I rob the thieves, and go merrily to London, it would be argument for a week, laughter for a month, and a good jest for ever.

POINS Stand close, I hear them coming.

They hide
Enter the thieves again

FALSTAFF Come my masters, let us share, and then to horse before day. If the Prince and Poins are not two arrant cowards there's no equity stirring. There's no more valour in that Poins than in a wild duck.

As they are sharing the Prince and Poins set upon them

PRINCE HAL Your money!
POINS Villains!

They all run away, Falstaff too, leaving the booty behind them

PRINCE HAL
Got with much ease. Now merrily to horse.
The thieves are all scattered and possessed with fear
So strongly that they dare not meet each other.
Each takes his fellow for an officer!
Away, good Ned! Falstaff sweats to death,
And lards the lean earth as he walks along.
Were it not for laughing I should pity him.
POINS How the fat rogue roared! *Exeunt*

SCENE III
Warkworth Castle.

Enter Hotspur reading a letter

HOTSPUR *But for my own part, my lord, I could be well contented to be there, in respect of the love I bear your house.*
He could be contented! Why is he not then? In respect of the love he bears our house? He shows in this he loves his own barn better than he loves our house. Let me see some more.
The purpose you undertake is dangerous,
Why, that's certain. 'Tis dangerous to take a cold, to sleep, to drink. But I tell you, my lord fool, out of this nettle, danger, we pluck this flower, safety.
The purpose you undertake is dangerous, the friends you have named uncertain, the time itself unsuitable,

and your whole plot too light, for the counterpoise of so great an opposition.

Say you so, say you so? I say unto you again, you are a shallow cowardly hind, and you lie. What a lack-brain is this! By the Lord, our plot is a good plot, as ever was laid, our friends true and constant. A good plot, good friends, and full of expectation. An excellent plot, very good friends. What a frosty-spirited rogue is this! Why, my Lord of York commends the plot, and the general course of the action. Zounds, if I were now by this rascal I could brain him with his lady's fan. Are there not my father, my uncle, and myself? Lord Edmund Mortimer, my Lord of York, and Owen Glendower? Is there not besides the Douglas? Have I not all their letters to meet me in arms by the ninth of the next month, and are they not some of them set forward already? What a pagan rascal is this, an infidel! Ha! You shall see now in very sincerity of fear and cold heart will he to the King, and lay open all our proceedings! O, I could divide myself, and go to buffets, for moving such a dish of skim milk with so honourable an action! Hang him, let him tell the King, we are prepared. I will set forward tonight.

Enter Lady Percy

How now, Kate? I must leave you within these two hours.

LADY PERCY

O my good lord, why are you thus alone?
For what offence have I this fortnight been
A banished woman from my Harry's bed?
Tell me, sweet lord, what is it that takes from you
Your stomach, pleasure, and your golden sleep?
Why do you bend your eyes upon the earth,
And start so often when you sit alone?

Why have you lost the fresh blood in your cheeks,
And given my treasures and my rights of you
To thick-eyed musing, and curst melancholy?
In your faint slumbers I by you have watched
And heard you murmur tales of iron wars,
Speak terms of còntrol to your bounding steed,
Cry 'Courage! To the field!' And you have talked
Of sallies, and retires, of trenches, tents,
Of palisades and frontiers, parapets,
Of basilisks, of cannon, culverin,[2]
Of prisoners' ransom, and of soldiers slain,
And all the currents of a heady fight.
Your spirit within you has been so at war,
And thus has so bestirred you in your sleep,
That beads of sweat have stood upon your brow
Like bubbles in a late-disturbèd stream.
And in your face strange motions have appeared,
Such as we see when men restrain their breath
On sudden behest. O, what portènts are these?
Some heavy business has my lord in hand,
And I must know it, else he loves me not.

HOTSPUR
What ho!

Enter a Servant

Has Gilliams with the packet gone?
SERVANT He has, my lord, an hour ago.
HOTSPUR Has Butler brought those horses from the sheriff?
SERVANT One horse, my lord, he brought even now.
HOTSPUR What horse? A roan, a crop-ear is it not?
SERVANT
It is, my lord.
HOTSPUR That roan shall be my throne.

---

[2]Large and small cannon.

Well, I will back him straight. O Esperance!
Bid Butler lead him forth into the park.

Exit Servant

LADY PERCY But hear you, my lord.

HOTSPUR What say you, my lady?

LADY PERCY What is it carries you away?

HOTSPUR Why, my horse, my love, my horse.

LADY PERCY
Out, you mad-headed ape!
A weasel has not such a deal of temper
As you are tossed with. In faith,
I'll know your business, Harry, that I will.
I fear my brother Mortimer does stir
About his title, and has sent for you
To line his enterprise. But if you go—

HOTSPUR
So far afoot I shall be weary, love.

LADY PERCY
Come, come, you parakeet, now answer me
Directly unto this question that I ask.
In faith, I'll break your little finger, Harry,
Now if you will not tell me all things true.

HOTSPUR
Away,
Away, you trifler! Love! I love you not,
I care not for you, Kate? This is no world
To play with puppets, and to tilt with lips.
We must have bloody noses, and cracked crowns,
And pass them current too. God's me! My horse!
What say you, Kate? What would you have with me?
What say you, Kate? What would you have with me?

LADY PERCY
Do you not love me? Do you not indeed?
Well, do not then, for since you love me not
I will not love myself. Do you not love me?
Nay, tell me if you speak in jest or no?

HOTSPUR

Come, will you see me ride?
And when I am a-horseback I will swear
I love you infinitely. But hark you, Kate,
I must not have you henceforth question me
Whither I go, nor reason whereabout.
Whither I must, I must. And, to conclude,
This evening must I leave you, gentle Kate.
I know you wise, but yet no farther wise
Than Harry Percy's wife. Constant you are,
But yet a woman. And for secrecy,
No lady closer, for I well believe
You will not utter—what you do not know.
And so far will I trust you, gentle Kate.

LADY PERCY

How? So far?

HOTSPUR

Not an inch further. But hark you, Kate,
Whither I go, thither shall you go too.
Today will I set forth, tomorrow you.
Will this content you, Kate?

LADY PERCY It must, of force. *Exeunt*

SCENE IV
East Cheap. The Boar's Head.

Enter Prince and Poins

PRINCE HAL Ned, pray come out of that fat room, and lend me your hand to laugh a little.

POINS Where have you been, Hal?

PRINCE HAL With three or four blockheads, among three or fourscore hogsheads. I have sounded the very bass string of humility. Man, I am sworn brother to a leash of drawers, and can call them all by their Christian names, as Tom, Dick, and Francis. They take it already upon their salvation that though I am but Prince of Wales yet I am the king of courtesy, and tell me flatly I am no proud Jack like Falstaff; but a Corinthian, a lad of mettle, a good boy—by the Lord, so they call me!—and when I am King of England I shall command all the good lads in Eastcheap. They call drinking deep 'dyeing scarlet', and when you breathe in your watering they cry 'Hem!' and bid you 'Play it off!' To conclude, I am so good a proficient in one quarter of an hour that I can drink with any tinker in his own language during my life. I tell you, Ned, you have lost much honour that you were not with me in this action. But, sweet Ned—to sweeten which name of Ned I give you this pennyworth of sugar, clapped even now into my hand by an understrapper, one that never spoke other English in his life than 'Eight shillings and sixpence', and 'You are welcome', with this shrill addition, 'Anon, anon, sir! Score a pint of sherry in the Half-moon!', or so. But Ned, to drive away the time till Falstaff comes—I pray do you stand in some by-room while I question my puny drawer to what end he gave me the sugar. And do you never leave calling 'Francis!', that his tale to me may be nothing but 'Anon'. Step aside, and I'll show you a precedent. *Exit Poins*

POINS (*within*) Francis!

PRINCE HAL You art perfect.

POINS (*within*) Francis!

Enter Francis, a Drawer

FRANCIS Anon, anon, sir. Look down into the Pomegranate, Ralph!

PRINCE HAL Come hither, Francis.

FRANCIS My lord?

PRINCE HAL How long have you to serve, Francis?

FRANCIS Truly, five years, and as much as to—

POINS (*within*) Francis!

FRANCIS Anon, anon, sir.

PRINCE HAL Five year! By our lady, a long lease for the clinking of pewter. But Francis, dare you be so valiant as to play the coward with your indenture, and show it a fair pair of heels, and run from it?

FRANCIS O Lord, sir, I'll be sworn upon all the books in England, I could find in my heart—

POINS (*within*) Francis!

FRANCIS Anon, sir.

PRINCE HAL How old are you, Francis?

FRANCIS Let me see, about Michaelmas next I shall be—

POINS (*within*) Francis!

FRANCIS Anon, sir—pray stay a little, my lord.

PRINCE HAL Nay, but hark you, Francis, for the sugar you gave me, it was a pennyworth, was it not?

FRANCIS O Lord, I would it had been two!

PRINCE HAL I will give you for it a thousand pound—ask me when you will, and you shall have it.

POINS (*within*) Francis!

FRANCIS Anon, anon.

PRINCE HAL Anon, Francis? No, Francis, but tomorrow, Francis. Or Francis, a-Thursday. Or indeed Francis, when you will. But Francis!

FRANCIS My lord?

PRINCE HAL Will you rob this leather-jerkin, crystal-button, crop-pated, agate-ring, puke-stocking, tape-garter, smooth-tongue Spanish pouch?

FRANCIS O Lord, sir, who do you mean?

PRINCE HAL Why then your brown sherry is your only drink. For look you, Francis, your white canvas doublet will sully. In Barbary, sir, it cannot come to so much.

FRANCIS What, sir?

POINS (*within*) Francis!

PRINCE HAL Away, you rogue, do you not hear them call?

Here they both call him; the Drawer stands amazed, not knowing which way to go
Enter Vintner

VINTNER What, stand you still and hear such a calling? Look to the guests within. *Exit Francis*
My lord, old Sir John with half-a-dozen more are at the door. Shall I let them in?

PRINCE HAL Let them alone awhile, and then open the door. *Exit Vintner*
Poins!

Enter Poins

POINS Anon, anon, sir.

PRINCE HAL Falstaff and the rest of the thieves are at the door. Shall we be merry?

POINS As merry as crickets, my lad. But hark you, what cunning match have you made with this jest of the drawer? Come, what's the issue?

PRINCE HAL I am now of all humours that have shown themselves humours since the old days of goodman Adam to the pupil age of this present twelve o'clock at midnight.

Enter Francis

What's o'clock, Francis?

FRANCIS Anon, anon, sir. *Exit*

PRINCE HAL That ever this fellow should have fewer words than a parrot, and yet the son of a woman! His industry is up-stairs and down-stairs, his eloquence the parcel of a reckoning. I am not yet of Percy's mind, the Hotspur of the North, he that kills some six or seven dozen of Scots at a breakfast, washes his hands, and says to his wife, 'Fie upon this quiet life, I want work.' 'O my sweet

Harry,' says she, 'how many have you killed today?' 'Give my roan horse a drench,' says he, and answers, 'Some fourteen,' an hour after, 'a trifle, a trifle'. I pray call in Falstaff. I'll play Percy, and that damned brawn shall play Dame Mortimer his wife. 'Right-ho!' says the drunkard. Call in Ribs, call in Tallow!

Enter Falstaff, Gadshill, Bardolph, and Peto; followed by Francis, with wine

POINS Welcome, Jack, where have you been?

FALSTAFF A plague of all cowards, I say, and a vengeance too, sure and amen! Give me a cup of sack, boy. Ere I lead this life long, I'll sew nether-stockings, and mend them and foot them too. A plague of all cowards! Give me a cup of sack, rogue. Is there no virtue extant?

He drinks

PRINCE HAL Did you never see Titan kiss a dish of butter—pitiful-hearted Titan!—that melted at the sweet tale of the sun's? If you did, then behold that compound.

FALSTAFF You rogue, here's lime in this sack too. There is nothing but roguery to be found in villainous man, yet a coward is worse than a cup of sack with lime in it. A villainous coward! Go your ways, old Jack, die when you will. If manhood, good manhood, is not forgotten upon the face of the earth, then am I a shotten herring. There live not three good men unhanged in England, and one of them is fat, and grows old. God help the while, a bad world I say. I would I were a weaver: I could sing psalms—or anything. A plague of all cowards, I say ever.

PRINCE HAL How now, woolsack, what mutter you?

FALSTAFF A king's son! If I do not beat you out of your kingdom with a dagger of lath, and drive all your subjects before you like a flock of wild geese, I'll never wear hair on my face more. You, Prince of Wales!

PRINCE HAL Why, you damned round man, what's the matter?

FALSTAFF Are not you a coward? Answer me to that—and Poins there?

POINS Zounds, you fat paunch, if you call me coward by the Lord I'll stab you.

FALSTAFF I call you coward? I'll see you damned ere I call you coward, but I would give a thousand pound I could run as fast as you can. You are straight enough in the shoulders, you care not who sees your back. Call you that backing of your friends? A plague upon such backing, give me them that will face me! Give me a cup of sack! I am a rogue if I drunk today.

PRINCE HAL O villain! Your lips are scarce wiped since you drunk last.

FALSTAFF All is one for that. (*He drinks*) A plague of all cowards, still say I.

PRINCE HAL What's the matter?

FALSTAFF What's the matter? There are four of us here have taken a thousand pound this day morning.

PRINCE HAL Where is it, Jack, where is it?

FALSTAFF Where is it? Taken from us it is. A hundred upon poor four of us.

PRINCE HAL What, a hundred, man?

FALSTAFF I am a rogue if I were not at half-sword with a dozen of them two hours together. I have escaped by miracle. I am eight times thrust through the doublet, four through the hose, my buckler cut through and through, my sword hacked like a handsaw—*ecce signum!*[3] I never dealt better since I was a man. All would not do. A plague of all cowards! Let them speak. If they speak more or less than truth, they are villains and the sons of darkness.

PRINCE HAL Speak, sirs, how was it?

---

[3]Here is the evidence.

GADSHILL We four set upon some dozen—

FALSTAFF Sixteen at least, my lord.

GADSHILL And bound them.

PETO No, no, they were not bound.

FALSTAFF You rogue, they were bound, every man of them, or I am a Jew else: a Hebrew Jew.

GADSHILL As we were sharing, some six or seven fresh men set upon us—

FALSTAFF And unbound the rest, and then come in the others.

PRINCE HAL What, fought you with them all?

FALSTAFF All? I know not what you call all, but if I fought not with fifty of them I am a bunch of radish. If there were not two or three and fifty upon poor old Jack, then am I no two-legged creature.

PRINCE HAL Pray God you have not murdered some of them.

FALSTAFF Nay, that's past praying for, I have peppered two of them. Two I am sure I have paid, two rogues in buckram suits. I tell you what, Hal, if I tell you a lie, spit in my face, call me horse. You know my old tactics—here I lay, and thus I bore my point. Four rogues in buckram let drive at me—

PRINCE HAL What, four? You said but two even now.

FALSTAFF Four, Hal, I told you four.

POINS Ay, ay, he said four.

FALSTAFF These four came all afront, and mainly thrust at me. I made no more ado, but took all their seven points in my buckier, thus!

PRINCE HAL Seven? Why, there were but four even now.

PRINCE HAL Seven? Why, there were but four even now.

FALSTAFF In buckram?

POINS Ay, four, in buckram suits.

FALSTAFF Seven, by these hilts, or I am a villain else.

PRINCE HAL Pray let him alone, we shall have more anon.

FALSTAFF Do you hear me, Hal?

PRINCE HAL Ay, and mark you too, Jack.

FALSTAFF Do so, for it is worth the listening to. These nine in buckram that I told you of—

PRINCE HAL So, two more already.

FALSTAFF Their points being broken—

POINS Down fell their hose.

FALSTAFF —began to give me ground. But I followed close, came in, foot and hand, and, with a thought, seven of the eleven I slew.

PRINCE HAL O monstrous! Eleven buckram men grown out of two!

FALSTAFF But as the devil would have it, three misbegotten knaves in Kendal green came at my back and let drive at me, for it was so dark, Hal, that you could not see your hand.

PRINCE HAL These lies are like their father that begets them, gross as a mountain, open, palpable. Why, you clay-brained guts, you knotty-pated fool, you obscene greasy tallow-catch—

FALSTAFF What, are you mad? Are you mad? Is not the truth the truth?

PRINCE HAL Why, how could you know these men in Kendal green when it was so dark you could not see your hand? Come, tell us your reason. What say you to this?

POINS Come, your reason, Jack, your reason!

FALSTAFF What, upon compulsion? Zounds, if I were at the torture, or all the racks in the world, I would not tell you on compulsion. Give you a reason on compulsion? If reasons were as plentiful as blackberries, I would give no man a reason upon compulsion, I.

PRINCE HAL I'll be no longer guilty of this sin. This sanguine coward, this bed-presser, this horse-back-breaker, this huge hill of flesh—

FALSTAFF God, you starveling, you eel-skin, you dried calf's-tongue, you bull's-pizzle, you cod-fish! O for breath to utter what is like you! You tailor's-yard, you sheath, you bow-case, you vile standing stick!

PRINCE HAL Well, breathe awhile, and then to it again, and when you have tired yourself in base comparisons hear me speak but this.

POINS Mark, Jack!

PRINCE HAL We two saw you four set on four, and bound them and were masters of their wealth—mark now how a plain tale shall put you down. Then did we two set on you four, and, with a word, out-faced you from your prize, and have it, yea, and can show it you here in the house. And Falstaff, you carried your guts away as nimbly, with as quick dexterity, and roared for mercy, and still ran and roared, as ever I heard bull-calf. What a slave are you to hack your sword as you have done, and then say it was in fight! What trick, what device, what starting-hole can you now find out, to hide you from this open and apparent shame?

POINS Come, let's hear Jack, what trick have you now?

FALSTAFF By the Lord, I knew you as well as he that made you. Why, hear you, my masters, was it for me to kill the heir apparent? Should I turn upon the true prince? Why, you know I am as valiant as Hercules. But beware instinct. The lion will not touch the true prince. Instinct is a great matter. I was now a coward on instinct. I shall think the better of myself, and you, during my life—I for a valiant lion, and you for a true prince. But by the Lord, lads, I am glad you have the money! Hostess, clap to the doors! Watch tonight, pray tomorrow! Gallants, lads, boys, hearts of gold, all the titles of good fellowship come to you! What, shall we be merry? Shall we have a play extempore?

PRINCE HAL Content, and the argument shall be your running away.

FALSTAFF Ah, no more of that Hal, if you love me.

Enter Hostess

HOSTESS O Jesu, my lord the Prince!

PRINCE HAL How now, my lady the Hostess, what say you to me?

HOSTESS Sure, my lord, there is a nobleman of the Court at door would speak with you. He says he comes from your father.

PRINCE HAL Give him as much as will make him a royal man and send him back again to my mother.

FALSTAFF What manner of man is he?

HOSTESS An old man.

FALSTAFF What does gravity out of his bed at midnight? Shall I give him his answer?

PRINCE HAL Pray do, Jack.

FALSTAFF Faith, and I'll send him packing. *Exit*

PRINCE HAL Now, sirs, by our lady, you fought fair, so did you, Peto, so did you, Bardolph. You are lions too, you ran away upon instinct, you will not touch the true prince, no, fie!

BARDOLPH Faith, I ran when I saw others run.

PRINCE HAL Faith, tell me now in earnest, how came Falstaff's sword so hacked?

PETO Why, he hacked it with his dagger, and said he would swear truth out of England but he would make you believe it was done in fight, and persuaded us to do the like.

BARDOLPH Yea, and to tickle our noses with spear-grass, to make them bleed, and then to beslubber our garments with it, and swear it was the blood of true men. I did that I did not this seven year before: I blushed to hear his monstrous devices.

PRINCE HAL O villain, you stole a cup of sack eighteen years ago, and were taken with the manner, and ever since you have blushed extempore. You had fire and sword on your side, and yet you ran away. What instinct had you for it?

BARDOLPH My lord, do you see these meteors? Do you behold these exhalations?

PRINCE HAL I do.

BARDOLPH What think you they portend?

PRINCE HAL Hot livers, and cold purses.

BARDOLPH Choler, my lord, if rightly taken.

PRINCE HAL No, if rightly taken, halter.

Enter Falstaff

Here comes lean Jack, here comes bare-bone. How now my sweet creature of bombast, how long is it ago, Jack, since you saw your own knee?

FALSTAFF My own knee? When I was about your years, Hal, I was not an eagle's talon in the waist—I could have crept into any alderman's thumb-ring. A plague of sighing and grief, it blows a man up like a bladder. There's villainous news abroad. Here was Sir John Bracy from your father. You must to the Court in the morning. That same mad fellow of the North, Percy, and he of Wales that gave Amamon the bastinado, and made Lucifer cuckold, and swore the devil his true liegeman upon the cross of a Welsh hook—what a plague call you him?

POINS O, Glendower.

FALSTAFF Owen, Owen, the same. And his son-in-law Mortimer, and old Northumberland, and that sprightly Scot of Scots, Douglas, that runs a-horseback up a hill perpendicular—

PRINCE HAL He that rides at high speed, and with his pistol kills a sparrow flying.

FALSTAFF You have hit it.

PRINCE HAL So did he never the sparrow.

FALSTAFF Well, that rascal has good mettle in him, he will not run.

PRINCE HAL Why, what a rascal are you then, to praise him so for running!

FALSTAFF A-horseback, you cuckoo, but afoot he will not budge a foot.

PRINCE HAL Yes, Jack, upon instinct.

FALSTAFF I grant you, upon instinct. Well, he is there too, and one Mordake, and a thousand Scots more. Worcester is stolen away tonight. Your father's beard is turned white with the news. You may buy land now as cheap as stinking mackerel.

PRINCE HAL Why then, it is likely if there comes a hot June, and this civil buffeting holds, we shall buy maidenheads as they buy hob-nails, by the hundreds.

FALSTAFF By the mass, lad, you say true, it is likely we shall have good trading that way. But tell me, Hal, are not you horribly afraid? You being heir apparent, could the world pick out three such enemies again, as that fiend Douglas, that spirit Percy, and that devil Glendower? Are you not horribly afraid? Does not your blood thrill at it?

PRINCE HAL Not a whit, in faith, I lack some of your instinct.

FALSTAFF Well, you will be horribly chidden tomorrow when you come to your father. If you love me, practise an answer.

PRINCE HAL Do you stand for my father and examine me upon the particulars of my life.

FALSTAFF Shall I? Content! This chair shall be my state, this dagger my sceptre, and this cushion my crown.

PRINCE HAL Your state is taken for a joint-stool, your golden sceptre for a leaden dagger, and your precious rich crown for a pitiful bald crown.

FALSTAFF Well, if the fire of grace is not quite out of you, now shall you be moved. Give me a cup of sack to make my eyes look red, that it may be thought I have wept, for

I must speak in passion, and I will do it in King Cambyses' vein.

PRINCE HAL Well, here is my leg.

FALSTAFF And here is my speech. Stand aside, nobility.

HOSTESS O Jesu, this is excellent sport, in faith.

FALSTAFF

Weep not, sweet Queen, for trickling tears are vain.

HOSTESS O the Father, how he holds his countenance!

FALSTAFF

For God's sake, lords, convey my tristful Queen,
For tears do stop the floodgates of her eyes.

HOSTESS O Jesu, he does it as like one of these harlotry players as ever I see!

FALSTAFF Peace, good pint-pot, peace, good ticklebrain.

(as KING*)*

Harry, I do not only marvel where you spend your time, but also how you are accompanied. For though the camomile, the more it is trodden on the faster it grows, yet youth, the more it is wasted the sooner it wears. That you are my son I have partly your mother's word, partly my own opinion, but chiefly a villainous trick of your eye and a foolish hanging of your nether lip that do warrant me. If then you are son to me—here lies the point—why, being son to me, are you so pointed at? Shall the blessed sun of heaven prove a truant, and eat blackberries? A question not to be asked. Shall the son of England prove a thief, and take purses? A question to be asked. There is a thing, Harry, which you have often heard of, and it is known to many in our land by the name of pitch. This pitch—as ancient writers do report—does defile, so does the company you keep. For, Harry, now I do not speak to you in drink, but in tears; not in pleasure, but in passion; not in words only, but in woes also. And yet there is a virtuous man whom I have often noted in your company, but I know not his name.

PRINCE HAL *(as himself)*
What manner of man, if it likes your Majesty?

FALSTAFF *(as* KING*)*
A goodly portly man, in faith, and a corpulent; of a cheerful look, a pleasing eye, and a most noble carriage; and, as I think, his age some fifty, or by our lady inclining to threescore. And now I remember, his name is Falstaff. If that man should be lewdly given, he deceives me; for, Harry, I see virtue in his looks. If then the tree may be known by the fruit, as the fruit by the tree, then peremptorily I speak it, there is virtue in that Falstaff. Him keep with, the rest banish. And tell me now, you naughty varlet, tell me where have you been this month?

PRINCE HAL Do you speak like a king? Do you stand for me, and I'll play my father.

FALSTAFF Depose me? If you do it half so gravely, so majestically, both in word and matter, hang me up by the heels for a rabbit-sucker, or a poulter's hare.

PRINCE HAL Well, here I am set.

FALSTAFF And here I stand. Judge, my masters.

PRINCE HAL *(as* KING*)*
Now, Harry, whence come you?

FALSTAFF *(as* HAL*)*
My noble lord, from Eastcheap.

PRINCE HAL *(as* KING*)*
The complaints I hear of you are grievous.

FALSTAFF *(as* HAL*)*
God's blood, my lord, they are false!
Nay, I'll tickle you for a young prince, in faith.

PRINCE HAL *(as* KING*)*
Swear you, ungracious boy? Henceforth never look on me. You are violently carried away from grace. There is a devil haunts you in the likeness of an old fat man, a

tun of man is your companion. Why do you converse with that trunk of humours, that sifting-hutch of beastliness, that swollen parcel of dropsies, that huge bombard of sack, that stuffed cloak-bag of guts, that roasted Manningtree ox with the pudding in his belly, that reverend Vice, that grey Iniquity, that Father Ruffian, that Vanity in years? Wherein is he good, but to taste sack and drink it? Wherein neat and cleanly, but to carve a capon and eat it? Wherein cunning, but in craft? Wherein crafty, but in villainy? Wherein villainous, but in all things? Wherein worthy, but in nothing?

FALSTAFF (*as* HAL)

I would your grace would take me with you. Whom means your grace?

PRINCE HAL (*as* KING)

That villainous abominable misleader of youth, Falstaff, that old white-bearded Satan.

FALSTAFF (*as* HAL)

My lord, the man I know.

PRINCE HAL (*as* KING)

I know you do.

FALSTAFF (*as* HAL)

But to say I know more harm in him than in myself were to say more than I know. That he is old, the more the pity, his white hairs do witness it; but that he is, saving your reverence, a whoremaster, that I utterly deny. If sack and sugar are a fault, God help the wicked! If to be old and merry is a sin, then many an old host that I know is damned. If to be fat is to be hated, then Pharaoh's lean kine are to be loved. No, my good lord! Banish Peto, banish Bardolph, banish Poins—but for sweet Jack Falstaff, kind Jack Falstaff, true Jack Falstaff, valiant Jack Falstaff—and therefore more valiant, being as he is old Jack Falstaff—banish not him your Harry's company, banish not him your Harry's company. Banish plump Jack, and banish all the world.

PRINCE HAL (*as* KING)
I do, I will.

Exeunt Hostess, Francis and Bardolph

Enter Bardolph, running

BARDOLPH O my lord, my lord, the sheriff with a most monstrous watch is at the door.

FALSTAFF Out, you rogue! Play out the play! I have much to say in behalf of that Falstaff.

Enter the Hostess

HOSTESS O Jesu, my lord, my lord!

PRINCE HAL Heigh, heigh, the devil rides upon a fiddle-stick. What's the matter?

HOSTESS The sheriff and all the watch are at the door. They are come to search the house. Shall I let them in?

FALSTAFF Do you hear, Hal? Never call a true piece of gold a counterfeit. You are essentially made without seeming so.

PRINCE HAL And you a natural coward without instinct.

FALSTAFF I deny your major. If you will deny the sheriff, so; if not, let him enter. If I become not a cart as well as another man, a plague on my bringing up! I hope I shall as soon be strangled with a halter as another.

PRINCE HAL Go hide behind the arras. The rest, walk up above. Now, my masters, for a true face, and good conscience.

FALSTAFF Both which I have had, but their date is out, and therefore I'll hide.

Exeunt all but the Prince and Peto

PRINCE HAL Call in the Sheriff.

Enter Sheriff and the Carrier

Now, master Sheriff, what is your will with me?

SHERIFF

First, pardon me, my lord. A hue and cry
Has followed certain men unto this house.

PRINCE HAL

What men?

SHERIFF

One of them is well known my gracious lord,
A gross fat man.

CARRIER As fat as butter.

PRINCE HAL

The man I do assure you is not here,
For I myself at this time have employed him.
And Sheriff, I will engage my word to you,
That I will by tomorrow dinner-time
Send him to answer you, or any man,
For anything he shall be chargèd with.
And so let me entreat you leave the house.

SHERIFF

I will, my lord. There are two gentlemen
Have in this robbery lost three hundred marks.

PRINCE HAL

It may be so. If he has robbed these men
He shall be answerable. And so, farewell.

SHERIFF

Good night, my noble lord.

PRINCE HAL

I think it is good morrow, is it not?

SHERIFF

Indeed, my lord, I think it is two o'clock.

Exit with Carrier

PRINCE HAL This oily rascal is known as well as Paul's.
Go call him forth.

PETO Falstaff! Fast asleep behind the arras, and snorting like a horse.

PRINCE HAL Hark how hard he fetches breath. Search his pockets.

Peto searches his pockets, and finds certain papers

What have you found?

PETO Nothing but papers, my lord.

PRINCE HAL Let's see what they are, read them.

PETO *Item a capon . . . . 2s. 2d.*
Item sauce . . . . 4d.
Item sack two gallons . . . . 5s. 8d.
Item anchovies and sack after supper . . . . . . 2s. 6d.
Item bread. . . . . ha'penny

PRINCE HAL O monstrous! But one halfpennyworth of bread to this intolerable deal of sack? What there is else keep close, we'll read it at more advantage. There let him sleep till day. I'll to the Court in the morning. We must all to the wars, and your place shall be honourable. I'll procure this fat rogue a charge of foot, and I know his death will be a march of twelve score. The money shall be paid back again with advantage. Be with me betimes in the morning, and so, good morrow, Peto.

PETO Good morrow, good my lord. *Exeunt*

Act III

SCENE I
Wales. Glendower's house.

Enter Hotspur, Worcester, Mortimer, and Glendower

MORTIMER
These promises are fair, the parties sure,
And our induction full of prosperous hope.

HOTSPUR
Lord Mortimer, and cousin Glendower, will you sit down?
And uncle Worcester. A plague upon it!
I have forgotten the map.

GLENDOWER No, here it is.
Sit, cousin Percy, sit—good cousin Hotspur—
For by that name as oft as Lancaster does speak of you
His cheek looks pale, and with a rising sigh
He wishes you in heaven.

HOTSPUR And you in hell,
As oft as he hears Owen Glendower spoken of.

GLENDOWER
I cannot blame him. At my nativity
The front of heaven was full of fiery shapes,
Of burning cressets, and at my birth
The frame and huge foundation of the earth
Shook like a coward.

HOTSPUR Why, so it would have done
At the same season if your mother's cat
Had but kittened, though yourself had never been born.

GLENDOWER
I say the earth did shake when I was born.
HOTSPUR
And I say the earth was not of my mind,
If you suppose as fearing you it shook.
GLENDOWER
The heavens were all on fire, the earth did tremble—
HOTSPUR
O, then the earth shook to see the heavens on fire,
And not in fear of your nativity.
Diseasèd nature oftentimes breaks forth
In strange eruptions, oft the teeming earth
Is with a kind of colic pinched and vexed
By the imprisoning of unruly wind
Within her womb; which for enlargement striving
Shakes the old beldam earth, and topples down
Steeples and moss-grown towers. At your birth
Our grandam earth, having this distemperature,
In passion shook.
GLENDOWER Cousin, of many men
I do not bear these crossings. Give me leave
To tell you once again that at my birth
The front of heaven was full of fiery shapes,
The goats ran from the mountains, and the herds
Were strangely clamorous to the frighted fields.
These signs have marked me extra-ordinary,
And all the courses of my life do show
I am not in the roll of common men.
Where is he living, clipped in with the sea
That chides the banks of England, Scotland, Wales,
Who calls me pupil or has read to me?
And bring him out that is but woman's son
Can trace me in the tedious ways of art,
And hold me pace in deep experiments.

HOTSPUR

I think there's no man speaks better Welsh.
I'll to dinner.

MORTIMER

Peace, cousin Percy, you will make him mad.

GLENDOWER

I can call spirits from the vasty deep.

HOTSPUR

Why, so can I, or so can any man:
But will they come when you do call for them?

GLENDOWER

Why, I can teach you, cousin, to command the devil.

HOTSPUR

And I can teach you, cousin, to shame the devil
By telling truth. Tell truth, and shame the devil.
If you have power to raise him, bring him hither,
And I'll be sworn I have power to shame him hence.
O, while you live, tell truth, and shame the devil!

MORTIMER

Come, come, no more of this unprofitable chat.

GLENDOWER

Three times has Henry Bolingbroke made head
Against my power; thrice from the banks of Wye
And sandy-bottomed Severn have I sent him
Bootless [fruitless] home, and weather-beaten back.

HOTSPUR

Home without boots, and in foul weather too!
How escapes he agues, in the devil's name?

GLENDOWER

Come, here is the map, shall we divide our right
According to our threefold order taken?

MORTIMER

The Archdeacon has divided it
Into three limits very equally.
England, from Trent and Severn hitherto,
By south and east is to my part assigned.

All westward, Wales beyond the Severn shore,
And all the fertile land within that bound,
To Owen Glendower. And, dear cousin, to you
The remnant northward lying off from Trent.
And our indentures tripartite are drawn,
Which being sealèd interchangeably—
A business that this night may execute—
Tomorrow, cousin Percy, you and I
And my good Lord of Worcester will set forth
To meet your father and the Scottish power,
As is appointed us, at Shrewsbury.
My father Glendower is not ready yet,
Nor shall we need his help these fourteen days.
(*To Glendower*) Within that space you may have drawn together
Your tenants, friends, and neighbouring gentlemen.

GLENDOWER

A shorter time shall send me to you, lords,
And in my conduct shall your ladies come,
From whom you now must steal and take no leave;
For there will be a world of water shed
Upon the parting of your wives and you.

HOTSPUR

I think my moiety, north from Burton here,
In quantity equals not one of yours.
See how this river comes cranking in,
And cuts me from the best of all my land
A huge half-moon, a monstrous cantle out.
I'll have the current in this place dammed up,
And here the smug and silver Trent shall run
In a new channel fair and evenly.
It shall not wind with such a deep indent,
To rob me of so rich a bottom here.

GLENDOWER

Not wind? It shall, it must—you see it does.

MORTIMER
Yes,
But mark how it bears its course, and runs up
With like advantage on the other side,
Gelding the opposèd continent as much
As on the other side it takes from you.
WORCESTER
Yes, but a little charge will trench him here,
And on this north side win this cape of land,
And then he runs straight and even.
HOTSPUR
I'll have it so, a little charge will do it.
GLENDOWER
I'll not have it altered.
HOTSPUR Will not you?
GLENDOWER
No, and you shall not.
HOTSPUR Who shall say me nay?
GLENDOWER
Why, that will I.
HOTSPUR
Let me not understand you then, speak it in Welsh.
GLENDOWER
I can speak English, lord, as well as you,
For I was trained up in the English Court;
Where being but young I framèd to the harp
Many an English ditty lovely well,
And gave the tongue a helpful ornament—
A virtue that was never seen in you.
HOTSPUR
Indeed, and I am glad of it with all my heart!
I had rather be a kitten and cry 'mew'
Than one of these same metre ballad-mongers.
I had rather hear a brazen candlestick turned,
Or a dry wheel grate on the axle-tree;
And that would set my teeth nothing on edge,

Nothing so much as mincing poetry.
'Tis like the forced gait of a shuffling nag.

GLENDOWER

Come, you shall have Trent turned.

HOTSPUR

I do not care, I'll give thrice so much land
To any well-deserving friend.
But in the way of bargain, mark you me,
I'll cavil on the ninth part of a hair.
Are the indentures drawn? Shall we be gone?

GLENDOWER

The moon shines fair, you may away by night.
I'll haste the writer, and with that
Break with your wives of your departure hence.
I am afraid my daughter will run mad,
So much she dotes now on her Mortimer. *Exit*

MORTIMER

Fie, cousin Percy, how you cross my father!

HOTSPUR

I cannot choose. Sometime he angers me
With telling me of the mole and the ant indeed,
Of the dreamer Merlin and his prophecies;
And of a dragon and a finless fish,
A clip-winged griffin and a moulting raven,
A couching lion and a ramping cat;
And such a deal of skimble-skamble stuff
As puts me from my faith. I tell you what—
He held me last night at least nine hours
In reckoning up the several devils' names
That were his lackeys. I cried 'Hum', and 'Well, go to!'
But marked him not a word. O, he is as tedious
As a tirèd horse, a railing wife,
Worse than a smoky house. I had rather live
With cheese and garlic in a windmill, far,
Than feed on dainties and have him talk to me
In any summer house in Christendom.

MORTIMER
In faith, he is a worthy gentleman,
Exceedingly well read, and profited
In strange concealments; valiant as a lion,
And wondrous affable, and as bountiful
As mines of India. Shall I tell you, cousin?
He holds your temper in a high respect
And curbs himself even of his natural scope
When you come across his humour, faith he does.
I warrant you that man is not alive
Might so have tempted him as you have done
Without the taste of danger and reproof.
But do not use it oft, let me entreat you.

WORCESTER
In faith, my lord, you are too wilful-blame,
And since your coming hither have done enough
To put him quite beside his patiènce.
You must needs learn, lord, to amend this fault.
Though sometimes it shows greatness, courage, blood—
And that's the dearest grace it renders you—
Yet oftentimes it does present harsh rage,
Defect of manners, want of government,
Pride, haughtiness, opinion, and disdain:
The least of which haunting a nobleman
Loses men's hearts and leaves behind a stain
Upon the beauty of all parts besides,
Beguiling them of commendatiòn.

HOTSPUR
Well, I am schooled—good manners be your luck!
Here come our wives, and let us take our leave.

Enter Glendower with the ladies

MORTIMER
This is the deadly spite that angers me,
My wife can speak no English, I no Welsh.

GLENDOWER
My daughter weeps, she will not part with you,
She'll be a soldier too, she'll to the wars.
MORTIMER
Good father, tell her that she and my aunt Percy
Shall follow in your conduct speedily.

Glendower speaks to her in Welsh, and she answers him in the same

GLENDOWER She is desperate here, a peevish, self-willed harlotry, one that no persuasion can do good upon.

The lady speaks in Welsh

MORTIMER
I understand your looks, that pretty Welsh
Which you pour down from these swelling heavens
I am too perfect in, and but for shame
In such a parley should I answer you.

The lady speaks again in Welsh

I understand your kisses, and you mine,
And that's a feeling disputatiòn.
But I will never be a truant, love,
Till I have learnt your language, for your tongue
Makes Welsh as sweet as ditties highly penned,
Sung by a fair queen in a summer's bower
With ravishing division to her lute.
GLENDOWER
Nay, if you melt, then will she run mad.

The lady speaks again in Welsh

MORTIMER

O, I am ignorance itself in this!

GLENDOWER

She bids you on the wanton rushes lay you down,
And rest your gentle head upon her lap,
And she will sing the song that pleases you;
And on your eyelids crown the god of sleep,
Charming your blood with pleasing heaviness—
Making such difference between wake and sleep
As is the difference betwixt day and night,
The hour before the heavenly-harnessed team
Begins his golden progress in the east.

MORTIMER

With all my heart I'll sit and hear her sing,
By that time will our book, I think, be drawn.

GLENDOWER

Do so, and those musicians that shall play to you
Hang in the air a thousand leagues from hence,
And straight they shall be here. Sit, and attend.

HOTSPUR

Come, Kate, you are perfect in lying down.
Come, quick, quick, that I may lay my head in your lap.

LADY PERCY Go, you giddy goose.

The music plays

HOTSPUR

Now I perceive the devil understands Welsh:
It is no marvel he is so humorous,
By our lady, he is a good musiciàn.

LADY PERCY

Then should you be nothing but musical,
For you are altogether governed by humours.
Lie still, you thief, and hear the lady sing in Welsh.

HOTSPUR I had rather hear Lady my hound howl in Irish.

LADY PERCY Would you have your head broken?

HOTSPUR No.
LADY PERCY Then be still.
HOTSPUR Neither, 'tis a woman's fault.
LADY PERCY Now, God help you!
HOTSPUR To the Welsh lady's bed.
LADY PERCY What's that?
HOTSPUR Peace, she sings.

Here the lady sings a Welsh song

Come, Kate, I'll have your song too.
LADY PERCY Not mine, in good sooth [truth].
HOTSPUR Not yours, in good sooth! Heart, you swear like a comfit-maker's wife—'Not you, in good sooth!', and 'As true as I live!', and 'As God shall mend me!', and 'As sure as day!'—
And give such silken surety for your oaths
As if you never walk further than Finsbury.
Swear me, Kate, like a lady as you are,
A good mouth-filling oath, and leave 'In sooth',
And such protest of pepper-gingerbread,
To velvet-trimmings, and Sunday citizens.
Come, sing.
LADY PERCY I will not sing.
HOTSPUR 'Tis the next way to turn tailor, or be redbreast teacher. If the indentures are drawn I'll away within these two hours. And so, come in when you will. *Exit*
GLENDOWER
Come, come, Lord Mortimer, you are as slow
As hot Lord Percy is on fire to go.
By this our book is drawn. We'll but seal,
And then to horse immediately.
MORTIMER With all my heart.
Exeunt

SCENE II
Westminster. The palace.

Enter the King, Prince Henry, and others

KING HENRY
Lords, give us leave. The Prince of Wales and I
Must have some private conference—but be near at hand,
For we shall presently have need of you. *Exeunt Lords*
I know not whether God will have it so
For some displeasing service I have done,
That in his secret sentence out of my blood
He'll breed revengement and a scourge for me.
But you do in your passages of life
Make me believe that you are only marked
For the hot vengeance and the rod of heaven,
To punish my mistreadings. Tell me else,
Could such inordinate and low desires,
Such poor, such bare, such lewd, such mean attempts,
Such barren pleasures, rude society,
As you are matchèd with, and grafted to,
Accompany the greatness of your blood
And hold their level with your princely heart?

PRINCE HAL
So please your majesty, I would I could
Quit all offences with as clear excuse
As well as, I am doubtless, I can purge
Myself of many I am chargèd with.
Yet such extenuation let me beg
As, in reproof of many tales devised,
Which oft the ear of greatness needs must hear,
By smiling tale-tellers, and base newsmongers,
I may for some things true. Wherein my youth
Has faulty wandered and irregular,
Find pardon on my true submissiòn.

KING HENRY

God pardon you! Yet let me wonder, Harry,
At your affections, which do hold a wing
Quite from the flight of all your ancestors.
Your place in Council you have rudely lost,
Which by your younger brother is supplied,
And are almost an alien to the hearts
Of all the Court and princes of my blood.
The hope and expectation of your time
Are ruined, and the soul of every man
Prophetically does forethink your fall.
Had I so lavish of my presence been,
So common-hackneyed in the eyes of men,
So stale and cheap to vulgar company,
Opinion, that did help me to the crown,
Had still kept loyal to possessiòn,
And left me in reputeless banishment,
A fellow of no mark nor likelihood.
By being seldom seen, I could not stir
But like a comet I was wondered at,
That men would tell their children, 'This is he!'
Others would say, 'Where, which is Bolingbroke?'
And then I stole all courtesy from heaven,
And dressed myself in such humility
That I did pluck allegiance from men's hearts,
Loud shouts and salutations from their mouths,
Even in the presence of the crownèd King.
Thus did I keep my person fresh and new,
My presence, like a robe pontifical,
Never seen but wondered at, and so my state,
Seldom, but sumptuous, showed like a feast,
And won by rareness such solemnity.
The skipping King, he ambled up and down,
With shallow jesters, and rash sputtering wits,
Soon kindled and soon burnt, lowered his state,
Mingled his royalty with capering fools,

Had his great name profanèd with their scorns;
And gave his countenance against his name
To laugh at gibing boys, and stand the push
Of every beardless vain comparative:
Grew a companion to the common streets,
Enfeoffed himself to popularity,
That, being daily swallowed by men's eyes,
They surfeited with honey, and began
To loathe the taste of sweetness, whereof a little
More than a little is by much too much.
So, when he had occasion to be seen,
He was but as the cuckoo is in June,
Heard, not regarded; seen, but with such eyes
As, sick and blunted with community,
Afford no extra-ordinary gaze—
Such as is bent on sun-like majesty
When it shines seldom in admiring eyes,
But rather drowsed and hung their eyelids down;
Slept in his face, and rendered such aspèct
As cloudy men use to their adversaries,
Being with his presence glutted, gorged, and full.
And in that very line, Harry, stand you,
For you have lost your princely privilege
With vile participation. Not an eye
But is a-weary of your common sight,
Save mine, which has desired to see you more,
Which now does that I would not have it do,
Make blind itself with foolish tenderness.

PRINCE HAL
I shall hereafter, my thrice-gracious lord,
Be more myself.

KING HENRY For all the world
As you are to this hour was Richard then
When I from France set foot at Ravenspurgh,
And even as I was then is Percy now.
Now by my sceptre, and my soul as well,

He has more worthy interest to the state
Than you the shadow of successiòn.
For of no right, nor colour like to right,
He does fill fields with harness in the realm,
Turns head against the lion's armèd jaws;
And being no more in debt to years than you
Leads ancient lords and reverend bishops on
To bloody battles, and to bruising arms.
What never-dying honour has he got
Against renownèd Douglas! Whose high deeds,
Whose hot incursions and great name in arms
Hold from all soldiers chief majority
And military title capital
Through all the kingdoms that acknowledge Christ.
Thrice has this Hotspur, Mars in swaddling clothes,
This infant warrior, in his enterprises
Discomfited great Douglas, taken him once,
Enlargèd him, and made a friend of him,
To fill the mouth of deep defiance up,
And shake the peace and safety of our throne.
And what say you to this? Percy, Northumberland,
The Archbishop's grace of York, Douglas, Mortimer,
Combine together against us and are up.
But wherefore do I tell these news to you?
Why, Harry, do I tell you of my foes,
Who are my nearest and dearest enemy?
You that are likely enough, through vassal fear,
Base inclination, and a fit of pique,
To fight against me under Percy's pay,
To dog his heels, and curtsy at his frowns,
To show how much you are degenerate.

PRINCE HAL

Do not think so, you shall not find it so;
And God forgive them that so much have swayed
Your majesty's good thoughts away from me!
I will redeem all this on Percy's head,

And in the closing of some glorious day
Be bold to tell you that I am your son;
When I will wear a garment all of blood,
And stain my features in a bloody mask,
Which, washed away, shall scour my shame with it.
And that shall be the day, whenever it lights,
That this same child of honour and renown,
This gallant Hotspur, this all-praisèd knight,
And your unthought-of Harry chance to meet.
For every honour sitting on his helm,
Would they were multitudes, and on my head
My shames redoubled. For the time will come
That I shall make this northern youth exchange
His glorious deeds for my indignities.
Percy is but my factor, good my lord,
To engross up glorious deeds on my behalf,
And I will call him to so strict account
That he shall render every glory up,
Yes, even the slightest worship of his time,
Or I will tear the reckoning from his heart.
This in the name of God I promise here,
Which if He be pleased I shall perform,
I do beseech your majesty may salve
The long-grown wounds of my intemperance.
If not, the end of life cancels all bonds,
And I will die a hundred thousand deaths
Ere break the smallest parcel of this vow.

KING HENRY

A hundred thousand rebels die in this.
You shall have charge and sovereign trust herein.

Enter Blunt

How now, good Blunt? Your looks are full of speed.

BLUNT

So has the business that I come to speak of.
Lord Mortimer of Scotland has sent word
That Douglas and the English rebels met
The eleventh of this month at Shrewsbury.
A mighty and a fearful head they are,
If promises be kept on every hand,
As ever offered foul play in a state.

KING HENRY

The Earl of Westmorland set forth today,
With him my son, Lord John of Lancaster,
For this advertisement is five days old.
On Wednesday next, Harry, you shall set forward.
On Thursday we ourselves will march.
Our meeting is Bridgnorth and, Harry, you
Shall march through Gloucestershire, by which account,
Our business valued, some twelve days hence
Our general forces at Bridgnorth shall meet.
Our hands are full of business, let's away,
Advantage feeds him fat while men delay.

Exeunt

Scene III
The Boar's Head.

Enter Falstaff and Bardolph

FALSTAFF Bardolph, am I not fallen away vilely since this last action? Do I not slim? Do I not dwindle? Why, my skin hangs about me like an old lady's loose gown. I am withered like an old apple. Well, I'll repent, and that suddenly, while I am in some liking. I shall be out of heart shortly, and then I shall have no strength to repent. If I have not forgotten what the inside of a church is made of, I am a peppercorn, a brewer's horse.

The inside of a church! Company, villainous company, has been the spoil of me.

BARDOLPH Sir John, you are so fretful you cannot live long.

FALSTAFF Why, there is it. Come, sing me a bawdy song, make me merry. I was as virtuously given as a gentleman need to be. Virtuous enough. Swore little. Diced not above seven times a week. Went to a bawdy-house not above once in a quarter—of an hour. Paid money that I borrowed—three or four times. Lived well, and in good compass: and now I live out of all order, out of all compass.

BARDOLPH Why, you are so fat, Sir John, that you must needs be out of all compass, out of all reasonable compass, Sir John.

FALSTAFF Do you amend your face, and I'll amend my life. You are our admiral, you bear the lantern in the poop, but it is in the nose of you. You are the Knight of the Burning Lamp.

BARDOLPH Why, Sir John, my face does you no harm.

FALSTAFF No, I'll be sworn, I make as good use of it as many a man does of a death's-head, or a *memento mori.* I never see your face but I think upon hell-fire, and Dives that lived in purple: for there he is in his robes, burning, burning. If you were any way given to virtue, I would swear by your face. My oath should be 'By this fire, that's God's angel!' But you are altogether given over, and were indeed, but for the light in your face, the son of utter darkness. When you ran up Gad's Hill in the night to catch my horse, if I did not think you had been a will-ò-the-wisp, or a ball of wildfire, there's no purchase in money. O, you are a perpetual triumph, an everlasting bonfire-light! You have saved me a thousand marks in links and torches, walking with you in the night between tavern and tavern. But the sack that you have drunk would have bought me lights as good cheap at the dearest chandler's in Europe. I have maintained that salamander of yours with fire any time this two-and-thirty years, God reward me for it!

BARDOLPH God, I would my face were in your belly!

FALSTAFF God-a-mercy! So should I be sure to be heartburnt.

Enter Hostess

How now, dame Partlet the hen, have you enquired yet who picked my pocket?

HOSTESS Why, Sir John, what do you think, Sir John, do you think I keep thieves in my house? I have searched, I have enquired, so has my husband, man by man, boy by boy, servant by servant—the tithe of a hair was never lost in my house before.

FALSTAFF You lie, hostess. Bardolph was shaved and lost many a hair, and I'll be sworn my pocket was picked. Go to, you are a woman, go!

HOSTESS Who, I? No, I defy you! God's light, I was never called so in my own house before.

FALSTAFF Go to, I know you well enough.

HOSTESS No, Sir John, you do not know me, Sir John, I know you, Sir John, you owe me money, Sir John, and now you pick a quarrel to beguile me of it. I bought you a dozen of shirts to your back.

FALSTAFF Canvas, filthy canvas. I have given them away to bakers' wives. They have made sieves of them.

HOSTESS Now as I am a true woman, holland of eight shillings an ell! You owe money here besides, Sir John, for your diet, and by-drinkings, and money lent you, four-and-twenty pound.

FALSTAFF He had his part of it, let him pay.

HOSTESS He? Alas, he is poor, he has nothing.

FALSTAFF How? Poor? Look upon his face. What call you rich? Let them coin his nose, let them coin his cheeks, I'll not pay a penny. What, will you make a youngster of me? Shall I not take my ease in my inn but I shall have my pocket picked? I have lost a seal-ring of my grandfather's worth forty marks.

HOSTESS O Jesu, I have heard the Prince tell him I know not how oft, that that ring was copper.

FALSTAFF How? The Prince is a Jack, a sneak-up. By God, if he were here I would cudgel him like a dog if he would say so.

Enter the Prince marching, with Peto, and Falstaff meets him, playing upon his truncheon like a fife

How now, lad? Is the wind in that door, in faith, must we all march?

BARDOLPH Yea, two and two, Newgate fashion.

HOSTESS My lord, I pray you hear me.

PRINCE HAL What say you, Mistress Quickly? How does your husband? I love him well, he is an honest man.

HOSTESS Good my lord, hear me.

FALSTAFF Pray let her alone, and listen to me.

PRINCE HAL What say you, Jack?

FALSTAFF The other night I fell asleep here, behind the arras, and had my pocket picked. This house is turned bawdy-house, they pick pockets.

PRINCE HAL What did you lose, Jack?

FALSTAFF Will you believe me, Hal, three or four bonds of forty pound apiece, and a seal-ring of my grandfather's.

PRINCE HAL A trifle, some eightpenny matter.

HOSTESS So I told him, my lord, and I said I heard your grace say so. And, my lord, he speaks most vilely of you, like a foul-mouthed man as he is, and said he would cudgel you.

PRINCE HAL What! He did not?

HOSTESS There's neither faith, truth, nor womanhood in me else.

FALSTAFF There's no more faith in you than in a stewed prune, and no more truth in you than in a drawn fox—and for womanhood, Maid Marian may be the deputy's wife of the ward to you. Go, you thing, go!

HOSTESS Say, what thing, what thing?

FALSTAFF What thing? Why, a thing to thank God on.

HOSTESS I am no thing to thank God on, I would you should know it. I am an honest man's wife, and setting your knighthood aside, you are a knave to call me so.

FALSTAFF Setting your womanhood aside, you art a beast to say otherwise.

HOSTESS Say, what beast, you knave, you?

FALSTAFF What beast? Why—an otter.

PRINCE HAL An otter, Sir John? Why an otter?

FALSTAFF Why? She's neither fish nor flesh, a man knows not where to have her.

HOSTESS You are an unjust man in saying so, you or any man knows where to have me, you knave, you.

PRINCE HAL You say true, hostess, and he slanders you most grossly.

HOSTESS So he does you, my lord, and said this other day you owed him a thousand pound.

PRINCE HAL Man, do I owe you a thousand pound?

FALSTAFF A thousand pound, Hal? A million, your love is worth a million, you owe me your love.

HOSTESS Nay my lord, he called you Jack, and said he would cudgel you.

FALSTAFF Did I, Bardolph?

BARDOLPH Indeed, Sir John, you said so.

FALSTAFF Yes, if he said my ring was copper.

PRINCE HAL I say it is copper, dare you be as good as your word now?

FALSTAFF Why Hal, you know as you are but man I dare, but as you are prince, I fear you as I fear the roaring of the lion's whelp.

PRINCE HAL And why not as the lion?

FALSTAFF The King himself is to be feared as the lion. Do you think I'll fear you as I fear your father? Nay, if I do, I pray God my girdle breaks.

PRINCE HAL O, if it should, how would your guts fall about your knees! But there's no room for faith, truth, nor honesty in this bosom of yours. It is all filled up with guts and midriff. Charge an honest woman with picking your pocket? Why, you impudent swollen rascal, if there were anything in your pocket but tavern reckonings, memorandums of bawdy-houses, and one poor pennyworth of sugar-candy to make you long-winded, if your pocket were enriched with any other injuries but these, I am a villain. And yet you will stand to it, you will not pocket up wrong! Are you not ashamed?

FALSTAFF Do you hear, Hal? You know in the state of innocency Adam fell, and what should poor Jack Falstaff do in the days of villainy? You see I have more flesh than another man, and therefore more frailty. You confess then, you picked my pocket?

PRINCE HAL It appears so by the story.

FALSTAFF Hostess, I forgive you, go make ready breakfast, love your husband, look to your servants, cherish your guests, you shall find me tractable to any honest reason, you see I am pacified—nay, pray be gone. *Exit Hostess* Now, Hal, to the news at Court: for the robbery, lad, how is that answered?

PRINCE HAL O my sweet beef, I must still be good angel to you—the money is paid back again.

FALSTAFF O, I do not like that paying back, 'tis a double labour.

PRINCE HAL I am good friends with my father and may do anything.

FALSTAFF Rob me the exchequer the first thing you do, and do it with unwashed hands too.

BARDOLPH Do, my lord.

PRINCE HAL I have procured you, Jack, a charge of foot.

FALSTAFF I would it had been of horse. Where shall I find one that can steal well? O for a ſine thief of the age of two-and-twenty or thereabouts! I am heinously unprovided. Well, God be thanked for these rebels, they offend none but the virtuous. I laud them, I praise them.

PRINCE HAL Bardolph!

BARDOLPH My lord?

PRINCE HAL

Go bear this letter to Lord John of Lancaster,
To my brother John, this to my Lord of Westmorland.

Exit Bardolph

Go, Peto, to horse, to horse, for you and I
Have thirty miles to ride yet ere dinner-time.

Exit Peto

Jack, meet me tomorrow in the Temple hall
At two o'clock in the afternoon.
There shall you know your charge, and there receive
Money and order for their furniture.
The land is burning, Percy stands on high,
And either we or they must lower lie. *Exit*

FALSTAFF

Rare words! Brave world! Hostess, my breakfast, come!
O, I could wish this tavern were my drum. *Exit*

Act IV

Scene I
The rebel camp near Shrewsbury.

Enter Hotspur, Worcester, and Douglas

HOTSPUR
Well said, my noble Scot! If speaking truth
In this fine age were not thought flattery,
Such attribution should the Douglas have
As not a soldier of this season's stamp
Should go as general current through the world.
By God, I cannot flatter, I do defy
The tongues of soothers, but a braver place
In my heart's love has no man than yourself.
Nay, task me to my word and prove me, lord.

DOUGLAS
You are the king of honour.
No man so potent breathes upon the ground
But I will beard him.

HOTSPUR Do so, and it is well.

Enter Messenger with letters

What letters have you there?—I can but thank you.

MESSENGER
These letters come from your father.

HOTSPUR
Letters from him? Why comes he not himself?

MESSENGER
He cannot come, my lord, he is grievous sick.
HOTSPUR
Zounds, how has he the leisure to be sick
In such a jostling time? Who leads his army?
Under whose government come they along?
MESSENGER
His letters bear his mind, not I my mind.
WORCESTER
I pray you tell me, does he keep his bed?
MESSENGER
He did, my lord, four days ere I set forth,
And at the time of my departure thence
He was much feared for by his physiciàns.
WORCESTER
I would the state of time had first been whole
Ere he by sickness had been visited.
His health was never better worth than now.
HOTSPUR
Sick now? Droop now? This sickness does infect
The very life-blood of our enterprise.
'Tis catching hither, even to our camp.
He writes me here that inward sickness—
And that his friends by deputation could not
So soon be drawn. Nor did he think it meet
To lay so dangerous and dear a trust
On any soul not sworn, but on his own.
Yet does he give us bold advertisement
That with our small conjunction we should on,
To see how fortune is disposed to us.
For, as he writes, there is no quailing now,
Because the King is certainly informed
Of all our purposes. What say you to it?
WORCESTER
Your father's sickness is a maim to us.

HOTSPUR
A perilous gash, a very limb lopped off—
And yet, in faith, it is not! His present want
Seems more than we shall find it. Were it good
To set the exact wealth of all our states
All at one cast? To set so rich a main
On the fine hazard of one doubtful hour?
It were not good, for therein should we read
The very bottom and the soul of hope,
The very limit, the very utmost bound
Of all our fortunes.

DOUGLAS
Faith, and so we should, where now remains
A sweet reversion—we may boldly spend
Upon the hope of what is to come in.
A comfort of retirement lives in this.

HOTSPUR
A rendezvous, a home to fly unto,
If now the devil and mischance look big
Upon the maidenhead of our affairs.

WORCESTER
But yet I would your father had been here.
The quality and lock of our attempt
Brook no division. It will be thought,
By some that know not why he is away,
That wisdom, loyalty, and mere dislike
Of our proceedings kept the Earl from hence.
And think how such an apprehensiòn
May turn the tide of fearful factiòn,
And breed a kind of question in our cause.
For well you know we of the offering side
Must keep aloof from strict arbitrament,
And stop all sight-holes, every loop from whence
The eye of reason may pry in upon us.
This absence of your father's draws a curtain

That shows the ignorant a kind of fear
Before not dreamt of.

HOTSPUR You strain too far.
I rather of his absence make this use.
It lends a lustre and more great opinion,
A larger dare to our great enterprise,
Than if the Earl were here. For men must think
If we without his help can make a head
To push against a kingdom, with his help
We shall o'erturn it topsy-turvy down.
Yet all goes well, yet all our joints are whole.

DOUGLAS
As heart can think. There is not such a word
Spoken in Scotland as this term of fear.

Enter Sir Richard Vernon

HOTSPUR
My cousin Vernon! Welcome, by my soul!

VERNON
Pray God my news be worth a welcome, lord.
The Earl of Westmorland seven thousand strong
Is marching hitherwards, with him Prince John.

HOTSPUR
No harm, what more?

VERNON And further, I have learned,
The King himself in person is set forth,
Or hitherwards intended speedily,
With strong and mighty preparatiòn.

HOTSPUR
He shall be welcome too. Where is his son,
The nimble-footed madcap Prince of Wales,
And his comrades that doffed the world aside
And bid it pass?

VERNON All furnished, all in arms,
All plumed like ostriches, that with the wind

Bated like eagles having lately bathed,
Glittering in golden coats like images,
As full of spirit as the month of May,
And gorgeous as the sun at midsummer,
Wanton as youthful goats, wild as young bulls.
I saw young Harry with his helmet on,
His armour on his thighs, gallantly armed,
Rise from the ground like feathered Mercury,
And vaulted with such ease into his seat
As if an angel dropped down from the clouds
To turn and wind a fiery Pegasus,
And witch the world with noble horsemanship.

HOTSPUR

No more, no more! Worse than the sun in March,
This praise does nourish agues. Let them come!
They come like sacrifices in their trim,
And to the fire-eyed maid of smoky war
All hot and bleeding will we offer them.
The mailèd Mars shall on his altar sit
Up to the ears in blood. I am on fire
To hear this rich reprisal is so nigh,
And yet not ours! Come, let me taste my horse,
Who is to bear me like a thunderbolt
Against the bosom of the Prince of Wales.
Harry to Harry shall, hot horse to horse,
Meet and never part till one drops down a corpse.
O that Glendower were come!

VERNON There is more news.

I learned in Worcester as I rode along
He cannot draw his force these fourteen days.

DOUGLAS

That's the worst tidings that I hear of yet.

WORCESTER

Ay, by my faith, that bears a frosty sound.

HOTSPUR

What may the King's whole army reach unto?

VERNON
To thirty thousand.
HOTSPUR Forty let it be.
My father and Glendower being both away,
The powers of us may serve so great a day.
Come, let us take a muster speedily.
Doomsday is near. Die all, die merrily.
DOUGLAS
Talk not of dying, I am out of fear
Of death or death's hand for this one half year.
Exeunt

SCENE II
A road near Coventry.

Enter Falstaff and Bardolph

FALSTAFF Bardolph, get you before to Coventry. Fill me a bottle of sack. Our soldiers shall march through. We'll to Sutton Coldfield tonight.

BARDOLPH Will you give me money, captain?

FALSTAFF Lay out, lay out.

BARDOLPH This bottle makes an angel.

FALSTAFF If it does, take it for your labour—and if it makes twenty, take them all, I'll answer the coinage. Bid my lieutenant Peto meet me at town's end.

BARDOLPH I will, captain. Farewell. *Exit*

FALSTAFF If I am not ashamed of my soldiers, I am a soused gurnet. I have misused the King's press damnably. I have got in exchange of a hundred and fifty soldiers three hundred and odd pounds. I press none but good householders, yeomen's sons; enquire out contracted bachelors, such as had been asked twice on the banns; such a commodity of warm slaves as had as soon hear the devil as a drum, such as fear the report of a musket worse than a struck fowl or a hurt wild duck. I pressed none but such toasts-and-butter, with hearts in their bellies no bigger than pins' heads, and they have bought out their services. And now my whole charge consists of ensigns, corporals, lieutenants, gentlemen of companies— slaves as ragged as Lazarus in the painted cloth, where the glutton's dogs licked his sores. And such as indeed were never soldiers, but discarded dishonest serving-men, younger sons to younger brothers, revolted tapsters, and ostlers trade-fallen; the cankers of a calm world and a long peace, ten times more dishonourable-ragged than an old frayed ensign. And such have I to fill up the rooms of them as have bought out their services, that you would think that I had a hundred and fifty tattered prodigals lately come from swine-keeping, from eating swill and husks. A mad fellow met me on the way, and told me I had unloaded all the gibbets and pressed the dead bodies. No eye has seen such scarecrows. I'll not march through Coventry with them, that's flat. Nay, and the villains march wide between the legs as if they had fetters on, for indeed I had the most of them out of prison. There's not a shirt and a half in all my company, and the half-shirt is two napkins tacked together and thrown over the shoulders like a herald's coat without sleeves. And the shirt, to say the truth, stolen from my host at Saint Albans, or the rednosed innkeeper of Daventry. But that's all one, they'll find linen enough on every hedge.

Enter the Prince and Westmorland

PRINCE HAL How now, blown Jack? How now, jacket?

FALSTAFF What, Hal! How now, mad wag? What a devil do you in Warwickshire? My good Lord of Westmorland, I cry you mercy, I thought your honour had already been at Shrewsbury.

WESTMORLAND Faith, Sir John, 'tis more than time that I were there, and you too; but my forces are there already. The King I can tell you looks for us all, we must away all night.

FALSTAFF Tut, never fear me, I am as vigilant as a cat to steal cream.

PRINCE HAL I think, to steal cream indeed, for your theft has already made you butter. But tell me, Jack, whose fellows are these that come after?

FALSTAFF Mine, Hal, mine.

PRINCE HAL I did never see such pitiful rascals.

FALSTAFF Tut, tut, good enough to toss, food for powder, food for powder, they'll fill a pit as well as better. Tush, man, mortal men, mortal men.

WESTMORLAND Ay, but Sir John, I think they are exceeding poor and bare, too beggarly.

FALSTAFF Faith, for their poverty I know not where they had that. And for their bareness I am sure they never learned that of me.

PRINCE HAL No, I'll be sworn, unless you call three fingers in the ribs bare. But man, make haste. Percy is already in the field. *Exit*

FALSTAFF What, is the King encamped?

WESTMORLAND He is, Sir John, I fear we shall stay too long. *Exit*

FALSTAFF Well,

To the latter end of a fray, and the beginning of a feast
Fits a dull fighter and a keen guest. *Exit*

SCENE III
The rebel camp.

Enter Hotspur, Worcester, Douglas, Vernon

HOTSPUR
We'll fight with him tonight.
WORCESTER It may not be.
DOUGLAS
You give him then advantage.
VERNON Not a whit.
HOTSPUR
Why say you so, looks he not for supply?
VERNON
So do we.
HOTSPUR His is certain, ours is doubtful.
WORCESTER
Good cousin, be advised, stir not tonight.
VERNON
Do not, my lord.
DOUGLAS You do not counsel well.
You speak it out of fear and cold heart.
VERNON
Do me no slander, Douglas. By my life,
And I dare well maintain it with my life,
If well-respected honour bids me on,
I hold as little counsel with weak fear
As you, my lord, or any Scot that this day lives.
Let it be seen tomorrow in the battle
Which of us fears.
DOUGLAS Yes, or tonight.
VERNON Content.
HOTSPUR
Tonight, say I.
VERNON
Come, come, it may not be. I wonder much,

Being men of such great leading as you are,
That you foresee not what impediments
Drag back our expedition. Certain horse
Of my cousin Vernon's are not yet come up,
Your uncle Worcester's horse came but today,
And now their pride and mettle are asleep,
Their courage with hard labour tame and dull,
That not a horse is half the half itself.

HOTSPUR

So are the horses of the enemy
In general journey-worn and so brought low.
The better part of ours are full of rest.

WORCESTER

The numbers of the King exceed now ours.
For God's sake, cousin, stay till all come in.

The trumpet sounds a parley
Enter Sir Walter Blunt

BLUNT

I come with gracious offers from the King,
If you permit me hearing and respect.

HOTSPUR

Welcome, Sir Walter Blunt: and would to God
You were of our determinatiòn!
Some of us love you well, and even those some
Envy your great deservings and good name,
Because you are not of our quality,
But stand against us like an enemy.

BLUNT

And God defend but ever I should stand so,
So long as out of limit and true rule
You stand against anointed majesty.
But to my charge. The King has sent to know
The nature of your griefs, and whereupon
You conjure from the breast of civil peace

Such bold hostility, teaching his duteous land
Audacious cruelty. If then the King
Has any way your good deserts forgotten.
Which he confesses to be manifold,
He bids you name your griefs. And with all speed
You shall have your desires with interest
And pardon absolute for yourself, and these
Herein misled by your suggestiòn.

HOTSPUR

The King is kind, and well we know the King
Knows at what time to promise, when to pay.
My father, and my uncle, and myself
Did give him that same royalty he wears.
And when he was not six-and-twenty strong,
Sick in the world's regard, wretched and low,
A poor unminded outlaw sneaking home,
My father gave him welcome to the shore.
And when he heard him swear and vow to God
He came but to be Duke of Lancaster,
To sue his heritage, and beg his peace
With tears of innocency and terms of zeal,
My father, in kind heart and pity moved,
Swore him assistance, and performed it too.
Now when the lords and barons of the realm
Perceived Northumberland did lean to him,
The more and less came in with cap and knee,
Met him in boroughs, cities, villages,
Attended him on bridges, stood in lanes,
Laid gifts before him, proffered him their oaths,
Gave him their heirs as pages, followed him
Even at the heels in golden multitudes.
He presently, as greatness knows itself,
Steps up a little higher than his vow
Made to my father while his blood was poor
Upon the naked shore at Ravenspurgh.
And now indeed takes on him to reform

Some certain edicts and some strait decrees
That lie too heavy on the commonwealth;
Cries out upon abuses, seems to weep
Over his country's wrongs. And by this face,
This seeming brow of justice, did he win
The hearts of all that he did angle for.
Proceeded further—then cut off the heads
Of all the favourites that the absent King
In deputation left behind him here,
When he was personal in the Irish war.

BLUNT

Tut, I came not to hear this.

HOTSPUR

Then to the point.
In short time after he deposed the King,
Soon after that deprived him of his life,
And in the neck of that taxed the whole state.
To make that worse, suffered his kinsman March—
Who is, if every owner were well placed,
Indeed his King—to be engaged in Wales,
There without ransom to lie forfeited.
Disgraced me in my happy victories,
Sought to entrap me by espìonage,
Berated my uncle from the Council-board,
In rage dismissed my father from the Court,
Broke oath on oath, committed wrong on wrong;
And in conclusion drove us to seek out
This head of safety, and with that to pry
Into his title, which we do find
Too indirect for long continuance.

BLUNT

Shall I return this answer to the King?

HOTSPUR

Not so, Sir Walter. We'll withdraw awhile.
Go to the King, and let there be impawned
Some surety for a safe return again.

And in the morning early shall my uncle
Bring him our purposes. And so, farewell.

BLUNT
I would you would accept of grace and love.

HOTSPUR
And may be so we shall.

BLUNT Pray God you do. *Exeunt*

SCENE IV
York. The Archbishop's palace.

Enter the Archbishop of York and Sir Michael

ARCHBISHOP
Hie, good Sir Michael, bear this sealèd brief
With wingèd haste to the Lord Marshàl,
This to my cousin Scroop, and all the rest
To whom they are directed. If you knew
How much they do import you would make haste.

SIR MICHAEL
My good lord,
I guess their tenor.

ARCHBISHOP Like enough you do.
Tomorrow, good Sir Michael, is a day
Wherein the fortune of ten thousand men
Must bide the touch. For, sir, at Shrewsbury,
As I am truly given to understand,
The King with mighty and quick-raisèd power
Meets with Lord Harry. And I fear, Sir Michael,
What with the sickness of Northumberland,
Whose power was in the first proportiòn,
And what with Owen Glendower's absence thence—
Who with them was a valued sinew too,
And comes not in, o'er-ruled by prophecies—

I fear the power of Percy is too weak
To wage an instant trial with the King.

SIR MICHAEL

Why, my good lord, you need not fear,
There are Douglas and Lord Mortimer.

ARCHBISHOP

No, Mortimer is not there.

SIR MICHAEL

But there are Mordake, Vernon, Lord Harry Percy,
And there is my Lord of Worcester, and a head
Of gallant warriors, noble gentlemen.

ARCHBISHOP

And so there is. But yet the King has drawn
The special head of all the land together.
The Prince of Wales, Lord John of Lancaster,
The noble Westmorland, and warlike Blunt,
And many more associates and dear men
Of estimation and command in arms.

SIR MICHAEL

Doubt not, my lord, they shall be well opposed.

ARCHBISHOP

I hope no less, yet needful it is to fear,
And to prevent the worst, Sir Michael, speed.
For if Lord Percy thrives not, ere the King
Disbands his army he means to visit us,
For he has heard of our confederacy,
And 'tis but wisdom to make strong against him.
Therefore make haste—I must go write again
To other friends. And so, farewell, Sir Michael.

Exeunt

Act V

SCENE I
The King's camp near Shrewsbury.

Enter the King, Prince Henry, Prince John,
Sir Walter Blunt, Falstaff

KING HENRY
How bloodily the sun begins to peer
Above yon bulky hill! The day looks pale
At its distemperature.
PRINCE HAL The southern wind
Does play the trumpet to its purposes,
And by its hollow whistling in the leaves
Foretells a tempest and a blustering day.
KING HENRY
Then with the losers let it sympathize,
For nothing can seem foul to those that win.

The trumpet sounds
Enter Worcester and Vernon

How now, my Lord of Worcester! It is not well
That you and I should meet upon such terms
As now we meet. You have deceived our trust,
And made us doff our easy robes of peace
To crush our old limbs in ungentle steel.
This is not well, my lord, this is not well.
What say you to it? Will you again unknit
The churlish knot of all-abhorrèd war,
And move in that obedient orb again

Where you did give a fair and natural light,
And be no more an exhaled meteor,
A prodigy of fear, and a portent
Of broachèd mischief to the unborn times?

WORCESTER

Hear me, my liege.
For my own part I could be well content
To entertain the lag end of my life
With quiet hours. For I protest
I have not sought the day of this dislike.

KING HENRY

You have not sought it? How comes it, then?

FALSTAFF Rebellion lay in his way, and he found it.

PRINCE HAL Peace, chatterer, peace!

WORCESTER

It pleased your majesty to turn your looks
Of favour from myself, and all our house,
And yet I must remember you, my lord,
We were the first and dearest of your friends.
For you my staff of office did I break
In Richard's time, and posted day and night
To meet you on the way, and kiss your hand,
When yet you were in place and in account
Nothing so strong and fortunate as I.
It was myself, my brother, and his son,
That brought you home, and boldly did outdare
The dangers of the time. You swore to us,
And you did swear that oath at Doncaster,
That you did nothing purpose against the state,
Nor claim further than your new-fallen right,
The seat of Gaunt, dukedom of Lancaster.
To this we swore our aid. But in short space
It rained down fortune showering on your head,
And such a flood of greatness fell on you,
What with our help, what with the absent King,
What with the injuries of a wanton time,

The seeming sufferances that you had borne,
And the contrarious winds that held the King
So long in his unlucky Irish wars
That all in England did repute him dead.
And from this swarm of fair advantages
You took occasion to be quickly wooed
To grip the general sway into your hand,
Forget your oath to us at Doncaster,
And being fed by us, you used us so
As that ungentle nestling the cuckoo's bird
Uses the sparrow—did oppress our nest,
Grew by our feeding to so great a bulk
That even our love durst not come near your sight
For fear of swallowing. But with nimble wing
We were enforced for safety sake to fly
Out of your sight, and raise this present force.
Whereby we stand opposèd by such means
As you yourself have forged against yourself,
By unkind usage, dangerous countenance,
And violation of all faith and troth
Sworn to us in your younger enterprise.

KING HENRY

These things indeed you have articulated,
Proclaimed at market crosses, read in churches,
To face the garment of rebelliòn
With some fine colour that may please the eye
Of fickle changelings and poor discontents—
Which gape and rub the elbow at the news
Of hurlyburly innovatiòn.
And never yet did insurrection want
Such water-colours to impaint its cause,
Nor moody beggars starving for a time
Of pell-mell havoc and confusiòn.

PRINCE HAL

In both your armies there are many a soul
Shall pay full dearly for this encounter

If once they join in trial. Tell your nephew,
The Prince of Wales does join with all the world
In praise of Henry Percy. By my hopes—
This present enterprise set off against—
I do not think a braver gentleman,
More active-valiant or more valiant-young,
More daring or more bold, is now alive
To grace this latter age with noble deeds.
For my part, I may speak it to my shame,
I have a truant been to chivalry,
And so I hear he does account me too.
Yet this before my father's majesty—
I am content that he shall take the odds
Of his great name and estimatiòn,
And will, to save the blood on either side,
Try fortune with him in a single fight.

KING HENRY

And, Prince of Wales, so dare we venture you,
Albeit considerations infinite
Do make against it. No, good Worcester, no,
We love our people well, even those we love
That are misled upon your cousin's part.
And will they take the offer of our grace,
Both he, and they, and you, yes, every man
Shall be my friend again, and I'll be his.
So tell your cousin, and bring me word
What he will do. But if he will not yield,
Rebuke and dread correction wait on us,
And they shall do their office. So, be gone.
We will not now be troubled with reply.
We offer fair, take it advisedly.

Exeunt Worcester and Vernon

PRINCE HAL

It will not be accepted, on my life.
The Douglas and the Hotspur both together
Are confident against the world in arms.

KING HENRY
Hence, therefore, every leader to his charge,
For on their answer will we set on them,
And God befriend us as our cause is just!
Exeunt all but the Prince and Falstaff

FALSTAFF Hal, if you see me down in the battle and bestride me, so. 'Tis a point of friendship.

PRINCE HAL Nothing but a Colossus can do you that friendship. Say your prayers, and farewell.

FALSTAFF I would it were bed-time, Hal, and all well.

PRINCE HAL Why, you owe God a death. *Exit*

FALSTAFF 'Tis not due yet—I would be loath to pay him before his day. What need I be so forward with him that calls not on me? Well, 'tis no matter, honour pricks me on. Yes, but how if honour pricks me off when I come on, how then? Can honour set to a leg? No. Or an arm? No. Or take away the grief of a wound? No. Honour has no skill in surgery then? No. What is honour? A word. What is in that word honour? What is that honour? Air. A trim reckoning! Who has it? He that died on Wednesday. Does he feel it? No. Does he hear it? No. 'Tis insensible, then? Yes, to the dead. But will it not live with the living? No. Why? Detraction will not suffer it. Therefore I'll none of it. Honour is a mere scutcheon. And so ends my catechism. *Exit*

SCENE II
The rebel camp.

Enter Worcester and Vernon

WORCESTER
O no, my nephew must not know, Sir Richard,
The liberal and kind offer of the King.

VERNON
It were best he did.
WORCESTER Then are we all undone.
It is not possible, it cannot be,
The King should keep his word in loving us.
He will suspect us ever, and find a time
To punish this offence in other faults.
Suspicion all our lives shall be stuck full of eyes,
For treason is but trusted like the fox,
Which never so tame, so cherished and locked up,
Will have a wild trick of his ancestors.
Look how we can or sad or merrily,
Interpretation will misquote our looks,
And we shall feed like oxen at a stall,
The better cherished ever the nearer death.
My nephew's trespass may be well forgotten,
It has the excuse of youth and heat of blood,
And an adopted name of privilege—
A hare-brained Hotspur, governed by a pique.
All his offences live upon my head
And on his father's. We did train him on,
And, his corruption being taken from us,
We as the spring of all shall pay for all.
Therefore, good cousin, let not Harry know
In any case the offer of the King.
VERNON
Deliver what you will; I'll say it is so.
Here comes your cousin.

Enter Hotspur and Douglas

HOTSPUR My uncle has returned;
Deliver up my Lord of Westmorland.
Uncle, what news?

WORCESTER
The King will bid you battle presently.
DOUGLAS
Defy him by the Lord of Westmorland.
HOTSPUR
Lord Douglas, go you and tell him so.
DOUGLAS
Certainly, and shall, and very willingly. *Exit*
WORCESTER
There is no seeming mercy in the King.
HOTSPUR
Did you beg any? God forbid!
WORCESTER
I told him gently of our grievances,
Of his oath-breaking—which he mended thus,
By now denying that he is forsworn.
He calls us rebels, traitors, and will scourge
With haughty arms this hateful name in us.

Enter Douglas

DOUGLAS
Arm, gentlemen, to arms! For I have thrown
A brave defiance in King Henry's teeth,
And Westmorland that was engaged did bear it,
Which cannot choose but bring him quickly on.
WORCESTER
The Prince of Wales stepped forth before the King,
And, nephew, challenged you to single fight.
HOTSPUR
O, would the quarrel lay upon our heads,
And that no man might draw short breath today
But I and Harry Monmouth! Tell me, tell me,
How showed his tasking? Seemed it in contempt?

VERNON

No, by my soul, I never in my life
Did hear a challenge urged more modestly,
Unless a brother should a brother dare
To gentle exercise and proof of arms.
He gave you all the duties of a man,
Trimmed up your praises with a princely tongue,
Spoke your deserving like a chronicle,
Making you ever better than his praise
By still dispraising praise valued with you.
And, what became him like a prince indeed,
He made a blushing recital of himself,
And chid his truant youth with such a grace
As if he mastered there a double spirit
Of teaching and of learning instantly.
There did he pause. But let me tell the world—
If he outlives the envy of this day,
England did never own so sweet a hope
So much miscònstrued in his wantonness.

HOTSPUR

Cousin, I think you are enamourèd
On his follies! Never did I hear
Of any prince so wild a liberty.
But be he as he will, yet once ere night
I will embrace him with a soldier's arm,
That he shall shrink under my courtesy.
Arm, arm with speed! And fellows, soldiers, friends,
Better consider what you have to do
Than I that have not well the gift of tongue
Can lift your blood up with persuasiòn.

Enter a Messenger

FIRST MESSENGER My lord, here are letters for you.

HOTSPUR I cannot read them now.
O gentlemen, the time of life is short!
To spend that shortness basely were too long
If life did ride upon a dial's point,
Still ending at the arrival of an hour.
And if we live, we live to tread on kings,
If die, brave death when princes die with us!
Now, for our consciences, the arms are fair
When the intent of bearing them is just.

Enter another Messenger

SECOND MESSENGER
My lord, prepare, the King comes on apace.

HOTSPUR
I thank him that he cuts me from my tale,
For I profess not talking. Only this—
Let each man do his best. And here draw I
A sword whose temper I intend to stain
With the best blood that I can meet with now
In the adventure of this perilous day.
Now, Esperance! Percy! and set on!
Sound all the lofty instruments of war,
And by that music let us all embrace,
For, heaven to earth, some of us never shall
A second time do such a courtesy.

Here they embrace, the trumpets sound

Exeunt

SCENE III
Plain between the camps.

The King enters with his army. Alarum. Then enter Douglas, and Blunt, disguised as the King

BLUNT
What is your name that in the battle thus
You cross me? What honour do you seek
Upon my head?
DOUGLAS Know then my name is Douglas,
And I do haunt you in the battle thus
Because some tell me that you are a king.
BLUNT
They tell you true.
DOUGLAS
The Lord of Stafford dear today has bought
Your likeness, for instead of you, King Harry,
This sword has ended him. So shall it you
Unless you yield you as my prisoner.
BLUNT
I was not born a yielder, you proud Scot,
And you shall find a king that will revenge
Lord Stafford's death.

They fight; Douglas kills Blunt
Then enter Hotspur

HOTSPUR
O Douglas, had you fought at Holmedon thus
I never had triumphed upon a Scot.
DOUGLAS
All's done, all's won. Here breathless lies the King.
HOTSPUR Where?
DOUGLAS Here.

HOTSPUR
This, Douglas? No, I know this face full well.
A gallant knight he was, his name was Blunt,
Semblably furnished like the King himself.

DOUGLAS
Ah fool, go with your soul, whither it goes!
A borrowed title have you bought too dear.
Why did you tell me that you were a king?

HOTSPUR
The King has many marching in his coats.

DOUGLAS
Now, by my sword, I will kill all his coats!
I'll murder all his wardrobe, piece by piece,
Until I meet the King.

HOTSPUR Up and away!
Our soldiers stand full fairly for the day. *Exeunt*

Alarum. Enter Falstaff alone

FALSTAFF Though I could escape shot-free at London, I fear the shot here: here's no scoring but upon the pate. Soft! Who are you? Sir Walter Blunt—there's honour for you! Here's no vanity! I am as hot as molten lead, and as heavy too. God keep lead out of me, I need no more weight than my own bowels. I have led my ragamuffins where they are peppered. There's not three of my hundred-and-fifty left alive—and they are for the town's end, to beg during life. But who comes here?

Enter the Prince

PRINCE HAL
What, stand you idle here? Lend me your sword.
Many a nobleman lies stark and stiff
Under the hoofs of vaunting enemies,

Whose deaths are yet unrevenged. I pray you
Lend me your sword.

FALSTAFF O Hal, I pray, give me leave to breathe awhile. Turk Gregory never did such deeds in arms as I have done this day. I have killed Percy, I have made him sure.

PRINCE HAL
He is indeed, and living to kill you.
I pray you, lend me your sword.

FALSTAFF Nay, before God, Hal, if Percy is alive you get not my sword, but take my pistol if you will.

PRINCE HAL Give it me. What, is it in the case?

FALSTAFF Ay, Hal, 'tis hot, 'tis hot. There's that will sack a city.

The Prince draws it out, and finds it to be a bottle of sack

PRINCE HAL
What, is it a time to jest and dally now?

He throws the bottle at him *Exit*

FALSTAFF Well, if Percy is alive, I'll pierce him. If he does come in my way, so. If he does not, if I come in his willingly, let him make a grilled rasher of me. I like not such grinning honour as Sir Walter has. Give me life, which if I can save, so. If not, honour comes unlooked for, and there's an end. *Exit*

SCENE IV
The same.

Alarum. Excursions. Enter the King, Prince Henry, Prince John, and Westmorland

KING HENRY
I pray, Harry, withdraw yourself, you bleed too much.
Lord John of Lancaster, go you with him.

LANCASTER
Not I, my lord, unless I did bleed too.

PRINCE HAL
I beseech your majesty, make up,
Lest your retirement does amaze your friends.

KING HENRY
I will do so. My Lord of Westmorland,
Lead him to his tent.

WESTMORLAND
Come, my lord, I'll lead you to your tent.

PRINCE HAL
Lead me, my lord? I do not need your help,
And God forbid a shallow scratch should drive
The Prince of Wales from such a field as this,
Where stained nobility lies trodden on,
And rebels' arms triumph in massacres!

LANCASTER
We breathe too long: come, cousin Westmorland,
Our duty this way lies: for God's sake, come.
Exeunt Lancaster and Westmorland

PRINCE HAL
By God, you have deceived me, Lancaster,
I did not think you lord of such a spirit.
Before, I loved you as a brother, John,
But now I do respect you as my soul.

KING HENRY
I saw him hold Lord Percy at the point
With lustier maintenance than I did look for
Of such an ungrown warrior.

PRINCE HAL O, this boy
Lends mettle to us all! *Exit*

Enter Douglas

DOUGLAS
Another king! They grow like Hydra's heads.
I am the Douglas, fatal to all those
That wear those colours on them. What are you
That counterfeit the person of a king?

KING HENRY
The King himself, who, Douglas, grieves at heart
So many of his shadows you have met,
And not the very King. I have two boys
Seek Percy and yourself about the field,
But seeing you fall on me so luckily
I will assay you—and defend yourself.

DOUGLAS
I fear you are another counterfeit,
And yet, in faith, you bear you like a king—
But mine I am sure you are, whoever you are,
And thus I win you.

They fight, the King being in danger; enter Prince Henry

PRINCE HAL
Hold up your head, vile Scot, or you are like
Never to hold it up again! The spirits
Of valiant Shirley, Stafford, Blunt are in my arms.
It is the Prince of Wales that threatens you,
Who never promises but he means to pay.

They fight; Douglas flees

Cheerily, my lord, how fares your grace?
Sir Nicholas Gawsey has for succour sent,
And so has Clifton—I'll to Clifton straight.

KING HENRY
Stay and breathe a while.
You have redeemed your lost opiniòn,
And showed you make tender care of my life
In this fair rescue you have brought to me.

PRINCE HAL
O God, they did me too much injury
That ever said I hearkened for your death.
If it were so, I might have let alone
The insulting hand of Douglas over you:
Which would have been as speedy in your end
As all the poisonous potions in the world,
And saved the treacherous labour of your son.

KING HENRY
Make up to Clifton, I'll to Sir Nicholas Gawsey. *Exit*

Enter Hotspur

HOTSPUR
If I mistake not, you are Harry Monmouth.

PRINCE HAL
You speak as if I would deny my name.

HOTSPUR
My name is Harry Percy.

PRINCE HAL Why then I see
A very valiant rebel of the name.
I am the Prince of Wales, and think not, Percy,
To share with me in glory any more.
Two stars keep not their motion in one sphere,
Nor can one England brook a double reign
Of Harry Percy and the Prince of Wales.

HOTSPUR

Nor shall it, Harry, for the hour is come
To end the one of us; and would to God
Your name in arms were now as great as mine.

PRINCE HAL

I'll make it greater ere I part from you,
And all the budding honours on your crest
I'll crop to make a garland for my head.

HOTSPUR

I can no longer brook your vanities.

They fight
Enter Falstaff

FALSTAFF Well said, Hal! To it, Hal! Nay, you shall find no boy's play here, I can tell you.

Enter Douglas; he fights with Falstaff, who falls down as if he were dead

Exit Douglas

The Prince mortally wounds Hotspur

HOTSPUR

O Harry, you have robbed me of my youth!
I better brook the loss of brittle life
Than those proud titles you have won of me.
They wound my thoughts worse than your sword my flesh.
But thoughts, the slaves of life, and life, time's fool,
And time, that takes survèy of all the world,
Must have a stop. O, I could prophesy,
But that the earthy and cold hand of death
Lies on my tongue. No, Percy, you are dust,

And food for—

He dies

PRINCE HAL

For worms, brave Percy. Fare you well, great heart!
Ill-weaved ambition, how much are you shrunk.
When this body did contain a spirit,
A kingdom for it was too small a bound.
But now two paces of the vilest earth
Are room enough. This earth that bears you dead
Bears not alive so stout a gentleman.
If you were sensible of courtesy
I should not make so dear a show of zeal,
But let my favours hide your mangled face,
And even in your behalf I'll thank myself
For doing these fair rites of tenderness.
Adieu, and take your praise with you to heaven!
Your ignominy sleep with you in the grave,
But not remembered in your epitaph.

He spies Falstaff on the ground

What, old acquaintance, could not all this flesh
Keep in a little life? Poor Jack, farewell!
I could have better spared a better man.
O, I should have a heavy miss of you
If I were much in love with vanity.
Death has not struck so fat a deer today,
Though many dearer, in this bloody fray.
Disbowelled will I see thee by and by,
Till then in blood by noble Percy lie. *Exit*

Falstaff rises

FALSTAFF Disbowelled? If you disbowel me today, I'll give you leave to powder me and eat me too tomorrow. God's blood, it was time to counterfeit, or that hot termagant

Scot had paid me, scot and lot too. Counterfeit? I lie, I am no counterfeit. To die is to be a counterfeit, for he is but the counterfeit of a man who has not the life of a man. But to counterfeit dying, when a man thereby lives, is to be no counterfeit, but the true and perfect image of life indeed. The better part of valour is discretion, in which better part I have saved my life. Zounds, I am afraid of this gunpowder Percy, though he is dead. How if he should counterfeit too and rise? By my faith, I am afraid he would prove the better counterfeit. Therefore I'll make him sure, yea, and I'll swear I killed him. Why may not he rise as well as I? Nothing confutes me but eyes, and nobody sees me. Therefore, man (*stabbing him*), with a new wound in your thigh, come you along with me.

He takes up Hotspur on his back. Enter Prince Henry and Prince John

PRINCE HAL
Come, brother John, full bravely have you fleshed
Your maiden sword.
LANCASTER But soft, whom have we here?
Did you not tell me this fat man was dead?
PRINCE HAL
I did, I saw him dead,
Breathless and bleeding on the ground. Are you alive?
Or is it fantasy that plays upon our eyesight?
I pray you, speak, we will not trust our eyes
Without our ears. You are not what you seem.

FALSTAFF No, that's certain, I am not a double-man. But if I am not Jack Falstaff, then am I a Jack. There is Percy!

He throws the body down

If your father will do me any honour, so. If not, let him kill the next Percy himself. I look to be either earl or duke, I can assure you.

PRINCE HAL Why, Percy I killed myself, and saw you dead.

FALSTAFF Did you? Lord, Lord, how this world is given to lying! I grant you I was down, and out of breath, and so was he; but we rose both at an instant, and fought a long hour by Shrewsbury clock. If I may be believed, so. If not, let them that should reward valour bear the sin upon their own heads. I'll take it upon my death, I gave him this wound in the thigh. If the man were alive, and would deny it, zounds, I would make him eat a piece of my sword.

LANCASTER This is the strangest tale that ever I heard.

PRINCE HAL This is the strangest fellow, brother John.
Come, bring your luggage nobly on your back.
(*Aside to Falstaff*) For my part, if a lie may do you grace,
I'll gild it with the happiest terms I have.

A retreat is sounded

The trumpet sounds retreat, the day is ours.
Come, brother, let us to the highest of the field,
To see what friends are living, who are dead.

Exeunt Prince of Wales and Lancaster

FALSTAFF I'll follow, as they say, for reward. He that rewards me, God reward him! If I do grow great, I'll grow less, for I'll purge, and leave sack, and live cleanly as a nobleman should do.

Exit, bearing off the body

SCENE V
The same.

The trumpets sound. Enter the King, Prince Henry, Prince John, Westmorland, with Worcester and Vernon prisoners

KING HENRY
Thus ever did rebellion find rebuke.
Ill-spirited Worcester, did not we send grace,
Pardon, and terms of love to all of you?
And would you turn our offers contrary?
Misuse the tenor of your kinsman's trust?
Three knights upon our party slain today,
A noble earl, and many a creature else
Had been alive this hour
If like a Christian you had truly borne
Between our armies true intelligence.

WORCESTER
What I have done my safety urged me to,
And I embrace this fortune patiently,
Since not to be avoided it falls on me.

KING HENRY
Bear Worcester to the death, and Vernon too;
Other offenders we will pause upon.
[*Exeunt Worcester and Vernon, guarded.*]
How goes the field?

PRINCE HAL
The noble Scot, Lord Douglas, when he saw
The fortune of the day quite turned from him,
The noble Percy slain, and all his men
Upon the foot of fear, fled with the rest;
And falling from a hill, he was so bruised
That the pursuers took him. At my tent
The Douglas is, and I beseech your grace
I may dispose of him.

KING HENRY With all my heart.

PRINCE HAL

Then, brother John of Lancaster, to you
This honorable bounty shall belong.
Go to the Douglas and deliver him
Up to his pleasure, ransomless and free.
His valors shown upon our crests to-day
Have taught us how to cherish such high deeds,
Even in the bosom of our adversaries.

PRINCE JOHN

I thank your grace for this high courtesy,
Which I shall give away immediately.

KING HENRY

Then this remains, that we divide our power.
You, son John, and my cousin Westmorland,
Towards York shall bend you with your dearest speed
To meet Northumberland and the prelate Scroop,
Who, as we hear, are busily in arms.
Myself and you, son Harry, will toward Wales
To fight with Glendower and the Earl of March.
Rebellion in this land shall lose its sway,
Meeting the check of such another day;
And since this business so fair is done,
Let us not leave till all our own be won. *Exeunt.*